W9-AQM-270

SAY YES TO WHAT'S NEXT

SAY YES TO WHAT'S NEXT

How to Age with Elegance and Class While
Never Losing Your Beauty and Sass

Lori Allen

with Kay Diehl

W PUBLISHING GROUP

AN IMPRINT OF THOMAS NELSON

Published in Nashville, Tennessee, by W Publishing Group, an imprint of Thomas Nelson.

Thomas Nelson titles may be purchased in bulk for educational, business, fundraising, or sales promotional use. For information, please e-mail SpecialMarkets@ ThomasNelson.com.

All Scripture quotations are taken from *The Holy Bible*, New International Version®, NIV®. © 1973, 1978, 1984, 2011 by Biblica, Inc.® Used by permission of Zondervan. All rights reserved worldwide.

Any Internet addresses, phone numbers, or company or product information printed in this book are offered as a resource and are not intended in any way to be or to imply an endorsement by Thomas Nelson, nor does Thomas Nelson vouch for the existence, content, or services of these sites, phone numbers, companies, or products beyond the life of this book.

Library of Congress Cataloging-in-Publication Data

Names: Allen, Lori, 1959- author.
Title: Say yes to what's next : how to age with elegance and class while never losing your beauty and sass! / Lori Allen with Kay Diehl.
Description: [Nashville] : W Publishing Group, [2020] | Includes bibliographical references. | Summary: "From the star of Say Yes to the Dress: Atlanta, now filming its eleventh season for TLC, comes a book and a life-makeover movement for women approaching fifty and beyond. Move over, girlfriend, Lori Allen is here to help you say yes to what's next! Lori uses her confidence, wisdom, and signature humor not only to help young brides on their most important day ever but also to model to them and their mothers how to live out the coming years as the best of their lives"— Provided by publisher.
Identifiers: LCCN 2020010587 (print) | LCCN 2020010588 (ebook) |
    ISBN 9780785234135 (hardcover) | ISBN 9780785234142 (ebook)
Subjects: LCSH: Middle-aged women—Health and hygiene. | Beauty, Personal. | Aging.
Classification: LCC RA778 .A4444 2020 (print) | LCC RA778 (ebook) | DDC
    646.7/2—dc23
LC record available at https://lccn.loc.gov/2020010587
LC ebook record available at https://lccn.loc.gov/2020010588

Printed in the United States of America

20 21 22 23 24   LSC   10 9 8 7 6 5 4 3 2 1

My grandmothers

My whole life I have been blessed to be surrounded
by a strong circle of women.
These women sewed their children's clothing
late into the night during the Depression
and encouraged their children to go to college when
that was unheard of.
I come from a long line of women who break barriers.

The generations of other strong women in my family

This book—and the cultural shift I pray it inspires—
is dedicated to the other women who came before me,
who stand beside me today, and who will come after me.
Jennie Ruth Baird, Lillis Harrison Burns,
Jean Baird Burns, Lucille Ryder Allen,
Mollie Allen Surratt, Becca Gunn Allen,
Caroline Jean Surratt, and Charlotte Jo Surratt.

My daughter, Mollie

Thank you, Mollie, for walking this journey with me.
From our first phone call about the idea for the book
until the hour we turned in the final manuscript, we did this together.
You have helped me pen my legacy, and it's been beyond special.

You

I wrote this book for you and for the millions of other women
who deserve their What's Next to be full of life, joy, and adventure.

Contents

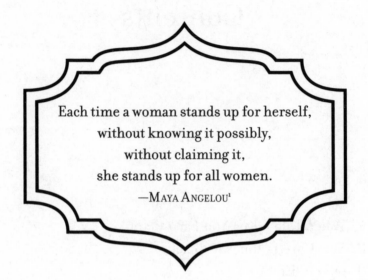

Each time a woman stands up for herself,
without knowing it possibly,
without claiming it,
she stands up for all women.

—MAYA ANGELOU[1]

Speak for Me

I was in Dallas for a big gala celebration, seated beside a very attractive woman who was about my age. Fashionably dressed, Texas-sized big hair, blonde. She was kinda quiet all through dinner, but I kept trying to chitchat with her—y'all know how I like to talk.

I told her about my store, Bridals by Lori, and about filming *Say Yes to the Dress: Atlanta* in the salon. I pointed across the table at Eddie, my husband. I bragged on my daughter, Mollie, and her husband, Jason, and my granddaughters, and about my son, Cory, his wife, Becca, and their newborn baby boy. She nodded as I was talking, but I could tell she wasn't really paying that much attention. That changed the minute I started telling her that I was writing this book about making the most of our remaining years. She suddenly came to life, explaining that her children were grown and that she'd been feeling adrift. She confessed that she didn't have a clear direction for going forward with her life, but she knew she didn't want to just put her feet up and wait for the sunset.

A plate of fancy cookies sat on the table in front of us, and I grabbed one. "The way I see it, life is a cookie," I told her, "and although nothing on this earth is promised, I still have about a quarter of my cookie left. It's sitting in the palm of my hand, and I intend to savor it all the way down to the crumbs. I want to go out full, having enjoyed every bite. I want my book to empower other women to do that as well."

As we stood up to leave the dinner, she grabbed me by both impeccably manicured hands and locked eyes with me. "Speak for me," she said earnestly. "Speak for me."

Her plea was so intense that it gave me a cold chill. In that moment, I felt a lot of weight on my shoulders, a duty to speak not just for her but for millions of women like us. I still do.

Who are we? We are women about to turn the page. We are no longer young, but we are not yet old. The soundtrack of our lives includes Faith Hill, Lionel Richie, David Bowie, and Whitney Houston. Our children are grown, flown, and on their own. Although we may still be plagued by hot flashes, we no longer have to buy Tampax—we can wear white pants without fear.

And there are a lot of us. We are a tribe that is forty million strong—emphasis on *strong*—but you'd never know it from how we are presented in the media.

Which is to say that we are not presented at all.

It's as if all of us went down with the *Titanic*—the movie. That film came out over twenty years ago, when we still were perceived as relevant. We are the women who have hidden away the vintage photos of our younger selves coiffed in poodle perms, shags, wedges, stick-straight hair parted down the middle, and bangs that fought with our eyelashes. We survived not just bad hair days but bad hair decades—not that anyone notices anymore. As far as popular culture is concerned, we died with our hairdos.

We've become invisible, which is a marketing mystery since

women our age have control over more than half of all discretionary income in the United States and 75 percent of our nation's wealth.[1] Despite being the healthiest, wealthiest, most accomplished generation of women in history, not much out there—unless it's CoQ10 or dental implants—is created with us in mind.

This ends now. The *What's Next* movement is dedicated to all of us who refuse to accept the idea that we no longer matter. We've got so much to offer, so much life left to live. It might be a very different life from the one we've been living—a new chapter is on the horizon. We have big plans—or we should have—but only if we make them.

It's our time. It's our turn. Let's talk about making the most of what's left of our cookie.

1

When Life Gives You Face-Plant

I'm hurt really bad, Monte."

Those were my last words before I blacked out. I was in my shop, Bridals by Lori. My best friend in the universe, Monte Durham, was with me. If you've watched *Say Yes to the Dress: Atlanta*, you'll already know that the two of us have a bond, a special connection.

We were in the salon, shooting opening scenes for the new season. It was a Wednesday. The store was closed, so there were no customers, just some of our staff, my son, Cory, the production crew, and Monte and me. I was in black, as I always am in the shop, and this particular sheath dress had a narrow pencil skirt with very little give at the bottom.

The scene we were filming called for some comic banter between us—Monte and I are the Sonny and Cher of TLC, and you already know which one of us is Cher. As I snapped at him for not taking better care of the merchandise, Monte was supposed to fling a dress at me. The dress chosen for the segment was an ivory Eve of Milady ball gown. It was gorgeous, with a fitted, embellished top and a billowy skirt consisting of five tiers of gossamer tulle over a glittery underlayer paved in sequins. It also had a very long train.

We were filming in the bridesmaids department, where there's a round display stand with three concentric steps, like a wedding cake. Usually there's a mannequin on it, but for the shoot, Monte was standing on the top, about two feet off the floor. He'd already whapped me in the face with the gown a few times, and we were cutting up. His ability to make me laugh is just one of the many reasons why I adore him, but everyone else on the set was in a good mood as well. Jen Holbach, our producer, had an idea for a great visual, and asked Monte for one more take. She had him hold the gown and spin around so she could capture the movement in slow motion. As he twirled, the tulle skirt floated through the air, and the camera caught the sparkle from the sequins underneath.

When the shot ended, I started walking past Monte in my three-inch Prada heels. I had no idea that the edge of the train was now fanned out over the bleached hardwood floor. The tulle was an exact match to the flooring, and it was absolutely invisible.

As soon as I stepped on it, I felt my left foot skid in front of my right. I had no traction at all. I might as well have been Tara Lipinski at center ice during the Olympics—wearing flip-flops smeared with bacon grease and WD-40. I began losing my balance. As I teetered, my inner voice shouted, *Drop to your knees, Lori!* It was advice welling up from deep in my childhood. As a kid, I'd been told over and over that once you knew you were going to fall, knees first was the best way to minimize the injury.

Monte was still on top of the pedestal. He reached out to grab me and keep me upright, but it was no use. Everything was happening too fast. As I went down, I instinctively put my arms out in front of me to break my fall, but they buckled under me. My entire body went *ker-splat* on the floor—hard. I landed face-first, then skidded another foot or so on the slippery train. I tried to push myself up with my hands, but I couldn't. I felt a warm trickle of blood streaming down my cheek, and then I lost consciousness.

Monte asked Janice, our bookkeeper, to call 911. Ashlen, who manages our bridesmaids department, grabbed somebody's coat and covered up my legs because she knew I wouldn't want to be sprawled out on the floor like that in front of the camera crew. She also says she took off my shoes, and Cory told me that Monte kissed me on the forehead as the EMTs were wheeling me out. I wouldn't know about any of that—I was still out cold.

I was unresponsive long enough that Monte and the others who saw me were afraid I'd broken my neck. I didn't come to until I was being transported to Northside Hospital. What brought me around was the siren, and the noise seemed both strange and familiar at the same time. It was loud, and I recognized what it was, but how weird to hear it from *inside* the ambulance—weirder still to know that it was wailing for me.

I woke up with the paramedics inches from my face. They were observing me closely, watching the pupils of my eyes, trying to assess whether I had some kind of brain injury. From the way they were hovering, I figured I might be in even worse shape than I already thought. What if the fall had shaken loose a blood clot? What if I had an aneurysm?

The idea that I might die before I got to the ER flitted across my traumatized brain, and I winced as I imagined the headline on my obituary.

Lori Allen, Star of *Say Yes to the Dress: Atlanta* since 2010,
Dies in Freak Accident in Her Sandy Springs Salon
Opened Bridals by Lori in 1980

How embarrassing—my demise due to a fall in my own shop because of the train on a bridal gown! How ironic! It would have been the punch line to the ultimate cosmic joke—here I was, writing this book about savoring the last quarter of my life-cookie, and maybe I'd just wolfed down the final bite.

Cory had followed the ambulance to the hospital in his own car and was with me as I was wheeled into the emergency room. The doctors took one look at me and called for X-rays. When the radiology technician asked me to raise my arms, I shook my head. I couldn't move them—at this point, I couldn't move much of anything, and it hurt just to breathe. The tech had to lift my arms for me, and I screamed out in pain.

Small wonder—as it turned out, both of my wrists were broken. So were three of my ribs. So was my nose. Mercifully, my neck was okay, but I did have a concussion and a nasty gash over my right eye. Even with all that, Northside didn't keep me overnight. There was no point because by now my upper body was so swollen that they couldn't tell what else might be broken. They stitched up the cut, immobilized my arms, and discharged me with orders to see an orthopedist as soon as possible.

I want to say that I looked like a hot mess leaving the ER, but truth be told, it wasn't even that good. I was wearing noisy, scratchy hospital paper pajamas, and I was as overinflated as a balloon in the Macy's Thanksgiving Day parade. With two shiners, a bent nose, casts on both arms, and stitches in my forehead, I could have frightened my own grandchildren on Halloween.

I felt as bad as I looked. They had to dope me up with so much morphine for the pain that my stomach was queasy. I threw up all the way home—and when you've got broken ribs, that's a new level of pain altogether. By the time my husband, Eddie, helped me through our front door, I was so miserable that he just plopped me into bed, paper pajamas and all.

I was fortunate that Dr. Bryce Gillespie, one of Atlanta's top hand surgeons, made time to see me the next morning. "Lori, your right wrist is shattered," he said. "Just setting it isn't going to be enough. To heal fully, you'll need at least two pins, maybe more. I may have to do surgery on the left hand as well, but let's take it one step at a time."

Dr. Gillespie operated a day later. He needed nine pins and a metal plate to stabilize the fracture and put the smithereens of my wrist back together. My daughter, Mollie, who'd been on holiday in Florida with her own family at the time of the accident, accompanied Eddie and me to the surgery. She had raced back to Atlanta as soon as she got the call from her brother.

That was against my orders—as hurt as I was, I was still as bossy as ever. I'd asked Cory not to contact her, which in hindsight doesn't make much sense, but I don't like worrying people. That's a trait that's hereditary—I got it straight from my daddy, and I didn't want Mollie to interrupt her vacation. I might have believed that I didn't need her to be there (and I now admit that I was wrong about that), but that's not the same thing as her need to be there for me. Putting myself in her place, if someone had tried telling me to stay on vacation after my mother had fallen, I wouldn't have listened either.

When we arrived for my surgery, we were greeted by some very familiar faces. The anesthetist had recently purchased her bridal gown at the salon, and one of my nurses had been a guest at Mollie's wedding. I was a bit worried about the operation, but it was very comforting to be surrounded by my family and some of my brides.

That was just the first of many blessings on a long road to recovery. The next came after Mollie, who handles my public relations with one hand and runs her own business with the other, put up a post on social media. She let fans of the show know what had happened to me and asked our followers for prayers on my behalf. That led to coverage by *USA Today*, *People* magazine, the *Today* show, AOL, Page Six, The Blast, and the *Atlanta Journal Constitution*. Heartfelt get-well wishes started pouring in from all over the world. At a time when I was at my lowest, I was lifted up by this giant wave of loving, healing energy, almost all of it from people I'd never met.

It's a very humbling experience to learn that so many people are praying for you, that they want you to feel better, and that they are taking the time to say they care about you. I'd been asking God for strength and for healing, and I realized that this was his response. God was returning my call, saying, *I got your message, Lori. It'll take a bit, but you're gonna be okay. Meanwhile, I'm sending in some backup. Hang in there.*

Gratitude washed over me. My belief in the power of prayer and my ability to connect with these godsends helped me stay upbeat, at least most of the time. It wasn't all sunshine and roses, though, and I did get to feeling sorry for myself, especially early on. My nose was as busted up as my wrist, and while I was having hand surgery, Mollie had the presence of mind to book a date with a plastic surgeon, Dr. John Connors. I got a nose job four days later. I told Dr. Connors that I didn't want him to make any changes, that I just wanted him to put my nose back the way it was and to make sure it would stay that way.

If I thought I looked scary when I left Northside that first night, that was nothing compared with how I looked now. With my right arm in a heavy black cast up to my elbow, two *very* black eyes, and a plastic face mask to protect my newly repaired beak, I looked like the blonde, banged-up second cousin of Darth Vader on a bad hair day, and it put me out of sorts.

I was especially ticked off when I realized that I'd have to miss Bridal Fashion Week in New York. It's a trip that Monte and I always look forward to, but now I was jealous. He was about to go off and have all that fun without me. I was so cranky that I was not particularly cordial—far from it—when ministers from our church paid a pastoral visit to the house.

How awful was I? They not only prayed for me, but they also thought it wise to ask the Lord to send Eddie some extra patience and heavenly comfort to help him put up with me while I was recuperating.

I was bruised and tender and grumpy, and I'm sure I was a terrible patient. I was also a tad loopy from the pain meds I was taking, but more than anything else, I was feeling helpless. The accident completely shut me down. For almost a month, there was nothing I could do for myself. During the first week, Mollie was with me 24/7. She had to feed me, bathe me, and brush my teeth, and with both arms in casts and my fingers swollen to the size of bratwursts, even deploying my own Charmin was beyond me. If we hadn't already owned one of those space-age wash-'n'-dry toilets with an electronically controlled bidet, I would have sent Eddie out to buy one.

Although I felt like crap—and looked like it too—I was confident that, underneath it all, I was strong, and that God had my back. Knowing that I'd recover, I pushed myself—within doctors' orders—to get back on my feet as soon as possible. And I was rewarded in a way I had not expected. As I began to feel better, all my senses were re-awakened, including my sense of wonder. I discovered that I had new eyes and ears—I marveled at the sounds of spring and at the explosion of blossoms on the trees. I also developed a rekindled appreciation for the everyday pleasures we take for granted—the aroma of freshly brewed coffee, and the ability to drink it from a cup, not through a straw—as they were restored to me one by one.

Through it all, my faith was always there, but the accident was a reminder of how fragile I was—how fragile we all are—and how life can change in an instant. The experience underscored the importance of living life to the fullest and of taking nothing for granted. I emerged with a new awareness of how precious life is and how essential the love of friends and family is in getting through each day.

I also found myself thinking back to those "what if" moments in the ambulance, when it occurred to me that I might be dying. I realized that if I keep wondering about that long enough, sooner or later I'm going to be right. The fall was a stark reminder that I'm not going to be here forever, and it helped me focus on what is truly important in my life. The question for me—for all of us—is what do we want to make of the rest of our time here?

WHAT'S NEXT
Girlfriends' Guide

- **Be Patient with Yourself When You're a Patient**

  Recovering from any serious injury or illness is never going to be a straight-line trajectory of continuous improvement. Inevitably, you will have setbacks. You will also have times when you're down in the dumps about these limitations on your life. Find your fighting spirit and look to your faith and your inner strength. You know it's there—look at how much it's gotten you through already.

- **Give Thanks for the Progress You're Making**

  Even if it's slower than you'd like. As we get older, bouncing back is going to take longer. Bones are slower to knit; black and blue marks stick around for weeks, not days. Focus on what you can do, not on what you can't do. Make the effort to feel better, and celebrate baby steps forward.

- **Appreciate the People Who Helped You Get Better**

  Everyone likes knowing that they're appreciated. I've never met medical staff who didn't welcome cookies or other goodies from a grateful patient. Gratitude warms the heart of both giver and recipient.

- **Little Things Mean a Lot**

  When you look better, you feel better. Plan some pampering into your recuperation. It doesn't have to be an outing, if you're not up to it. Even a foot rub from your spouse, a manicure with a friend, or a new pair of pj's will lift your spirits.

- ## Take the Time to Look Around

    You know how much more you notice about what's around you when you're walking instead of driving in a car? Do that now while you're slow. Listen for birdsongs, or watch the kids playing in the park, or check out how much some people really *do* start looking like their pets.

- ## A Little Introspection Is in Order

    While you're on the mend, you may not be functioning at 100 percent, but that doesn't mean you can't put this time to good use. For the moment you are your own captive audience, so while your body is limited, let your imagination soar. This is a great opportunity to take a good look at what's left of your cookie. What do you want your life to be five years from now? Ten years from now? Are there trips you want to take, business opportunities you'd like to pursue, a foreign language you'd like to master? How are you going to make that life happen? Set some goals and figure out a path toward achieving them.

2

Self-Care Is the New Black

Self-care runs deep in my family—I come from a long line of women who take pride in their appearance. At the age of eighty-six, my mother still goes every three weeks to get her hair done, and every two weeks for a manicure and pedicure. Her mother—my grandmother Baird—was the same way. She was raised in a well-to-do family, and even though the Depression wiped them out financially, it never stopped being important to her to look good. Each Sunday, she'd put on her best dress—even if it was one that she had sewn herself—to go to church. And her pearls and a hat.

My childhood memory of my grandmother is that she always made the effort to be stylish and well-groomed, and that's how I think of her to this day. That's also how I'd like my own grandchildren to think of me now. I want them to say, "That's my grandmother, Bella! Doesn't she look great? Bella is awesome." When my kids were growing up, I cared a lot about making sure that Cory and Mollie were proud of me. I was as frazzled as other working moms, but I kept the image of my mother and grandmother in my head. Owning Bridals by Lori helped too. I had to look good in the salon every day—my name was on the building, and I had to represent my business well.

It's no different now, except for the frazzled part. I still want my kids and grandkids to appreciate that I value myself enough to put some effort into how I look—it's something that matters a lot to me.

Underlying this desire is a basic truth: the esteem we seek from others must start with self-esteem. Babies will love you no matter what, but as they get older, you want them to look up to you and respect you, and that begins with their bedrock understanding that you respect yourself.

In the salon I see women every day who don't do that. Often it's the mother of the bride. She's just spent $5,000 on a stunning couture gown for her daughter but won't spend even 10 percent of that on herself. Instead, she makes a beeline for the sale rack, searching for the least expensive dress she can find.

Why? Because she doesn't see herself as important. Because she doesn't see herself, period.

We struggle to help her find a gown. Odds are that she's put off shopping for it, and now she's a bit panic-stricken. Even on a tight budget, she's finicky and will tell me in great detail what's wrong with the neckline of the dress. Or the tummy area, or the hips. But that's not really the problem. This mother of the bride is unhappy, not with the dress, but with the body that's in it—her own—because she's been putting herself last most of her life. In the process of taking care of everyone else, she's let herself go, and now she's upset that there's not enough time before her daughter's wedding to make up for all that neglect.

When did that start? When did she make the unconscious decision that she was not important? Most women in their teens and twenties care a great deal about their appearance and devote a lot of time and energy to it.

What happened? I already know, and so do you. Children and family happened. Women are givers—we tend to put ourselves last for the sake of our families. We give and give and give until we're as squozen out as an empty toothpaste tube, and there's nothing left.

Neglecting yourself is a slippery slope, and you take that first step downhill on the day you leave the maternity ward—when you find out firsthand that parenting is a roller-coaster ride, and that your time is no longer your own. Your priorities take a back seat to caring for your infant.

Out of sheer self-defense you learn to shower and dress faster than you ever thought possible. You put your hair in a ponytail, grab the least wrinkled pants out of the dryer or off the mountain of clothes on the chair, and go.

It's no better with toddlers and preschoolers. That roller coaster speeds up—pandemonium can break out at any moment. You don't dare have a soak in the tub while the children are awake, for fear that they'll undertake a science experiment to see what happens when they vacuum the water out of the dog dish, then poke their wet fingers into a light socket.

When you're careening from one crisis to another, day after day, it's easy to believe that it doesn't matter what you look like. And besides, money is tight. Maybe you and your husband are saving for a down payment on a house or for adding a second bathroom. If he's the primary wage earner, he has to be well dressed for his job. You figure that his appearance is more important than you looking presentable while you're working part-time from home or driving your kids for playgroup or carpool.

And you're beat—bone weary. Motherhood is exhausting. At eight o'clock, or as soon as you've read your kids *Bedtime for Frances*—twice—your own head is on the pillow. During this phase of life, self-care looks a lot like sleep, and you never get enough of it. My daughter, Mollie, and my daughter-in-law, Becca, are in this phase now, and both of them are always on the hunt for industrial-strength undereye concealer.

By the time the children are old enough to go to school, society has taught us to equate our own self-esteem with how well they are doing. Their success is our yardstick—it's how we know whether we're doing a good job of mothering. We want them to be happy, and we want to expand their horizons. Feeling guilty about buying something for ourselves when there's club soccer, cheerleading, and tuba lessons to pay for becomes almost second nature. Eventually, it almost feels like stealing.

We tend to reinforce this attitude when we gossip among ourselves about other women. If you ever hear someone say, "Oh, she spends a lot on herself," you can be sure that it's not meant as a compliment. Actually, it's worse—it's an accusation. Looking good is taken as proof positive that a woman has her priorities screwed up and is selfishly putting her own wants and needs ahead of those of her family.

Sooner or later there's a price to pay, and you're it. Self-sacrifice may sound noble, but there's nothing heroic about it. As our children grow, we lose the women we used to be. Worse yet, we start losing our dreams of the women we had wanted to become.

In short, we lose us.

By the time the nest is empty, too many of us are no longer proud of ourselves. When we look in the mirror, we don't like what we see, or who we see, so we stop looking. And then we decide that it's hopeless. After twenty-plus years of deferred maintenance, we compare ourselves with the polished, airbrushed images of younger women in magazines, figure we're too far gone, and just flat out give up.

If that sounds familiar, I want to nudge you out of that mindset. I'm taking it upon myself to push you to "un-give up."

You have a lot in common with that mother of the bride I see every day—the one who has convinced herself that the only dress she deserves is one on deep discount. You've marked yourself down, and it's time to remedy that. It's time to get back to being your best self—not to look good for your child's wedding but for your own sake.

Self-care is not self-indulgence. It's not a frivolous expense. Get your keister off the clearance rack and treat yourself like you belong in the glass showcase—where they keep the good stuff. The way I look at it, you can't afford not to take care of you. Why? Those hair-color commercials have been preaching this truth for generations: "because you're worth it."

God says that we are all valuable, that all of us are important. And we've got to take care of what God thinks is valuable—even when it's you.

Especially when it's you. I want you to fall back into the habit of taking good care of yourself, to fall back into the mindset you had when you were eighteen. Not because you're trying to look eighteen again, but because you are determined to reclaim your power and become the best version of yourself as you head into this next chapter of your life.

How do you do that? Baby steps, little by little.

Skin Care

You might begin with your skin. I used to work at the country club pool in high school, and I lifeguarded in college. During the summers, I lived outside. I coated my nose with zinc oxide as I sat in that tall white chair overlooking the pool, but the rest of me was slathered with baby oil, which acted like a magnifying glass for the sun's ultraviolet rays. I even had one of those cardboard fold-up reflectors lined with tinfoil. The idea was to hold it in front of your chest and face to get more tanning power out of each minute in the sun. And of course I spritzed my hair with Sun In to get the perfect shade of orange!

Nobody knew about SPF anything back then. We just knew it was cool to have a good tan. I could easily have ended up as corrugated and leathery as an alligator handbag, and I'm very fortunate that I'm not eaten up with skin cancer. I now apply sunscreen daily, but I do have a ton of freckles and liver spots as souvenirs from the tanning habits of my youth.

Skin care can be pricey, and I suspect that if you bought all the latest goops and slathers recommended in the beauty and fashion magazines, you could go broke taking care of your face, neck, and décolletage. You don't have to do that—you certainly can find effective less costly products that will improve the appearance of your skin. I'm not going to advise you on what to use, but I am going to suggest a visit to your dermatologist to discuss the best course of treatment for your skin type. If your daily skin care program doesn't already include them, plan to start using at least a cleanser, a moisturizer, a sunscreen, and a wrinkle fighter. And ditch the guilt—a regular exfoliating facial is not an extravagance. It doesn't have to come from an aesthetician at a spa or salon. You can buy yourself one at the drugstore.

If you have age spots and wrinkles, you have many options, including a variety of laser treatments. At some point the possibility of plastic surgery may come up. This is another arena where women can be terribly snippy about one another. "Oh, she had this done and that done."

Stop it. It's catty, and it's behind-the-back nasty. Why can't we be happy for another member of our tribe? Why can't we say, "She had a little work done. Dang, she looks good! Who'd she go to?"

I have no problem talking about my own face-lift. As Monte is fond of saying, I've got more plastic than a Tupperware party. A few years ago I had an honesty hour with my looking glass. I saw this stranger looking back at me, and I didn't like her at all. I flung accusations at my reflection—that girl in the bathroom mirror was looking worn-out and haggard.

Two years after a major surgery—more about that in the next chapter—I was finally starting to feel like myself, but I still looked awful. I went to Atlanta's preeminent plastic surgeon, Dr. John Connors, and asked him what I could do. (He's the same doctor who repaired my broken nose after my face-plant in the salon.) I made it clear to him that I wasn't after any radical transformation. "Some women end up so stretched and tight that they're unrecognizable," I said. "I don't want that. I just want to look rested and fresh, like I've been on a great vacation."

He understood, and on the episodes of *Say Yes* that were filmed after my face-lift, very few viewers noticed. People just thought that I was finally looking better after my surgery. Close friends and family were incredibly supportive, but I did get a little push-back from some folks who didn't know me very well. They all had the same question: "After all you've been through, why did you do that?"

"You answered your own question as you were asking it," I told them. "It's *because* of all I've been through."

I wanted to look as healthy on the outside as I felt on the inside. I felt victorious after beating back a serious health challenge, but not everyone is going to react the same way. For me, plastic surgery was a rejuvenating investment in myself, and it made all the difference.

That choice is yours alone to make. If you want a face-lift, go for it. Own it, and don't let others judge you for it. Do whatever it takes for you to be your best version of yourself, to make your own peace with the girl in the mirror.

Hair—on Your Head

How long have you been wearing the same hairstyle? More and more of your hair is coming in gray, which tends to be fine and dry, whether you color it or not. Does your style work with that new texture? If you've gained or lost weight, is it still the best cut for the changing contours of your face?

I'd had the same short coif for the first decade that *Say Yes* was on the air, but when I decided to grow it out, I was not prepared for the hubbub that ensued. On my social media pages, my new hairdo was Topic A of conversation for months. I like the way I look with longer hair, and the consensus of opinion seems to be that it makes me look younger—so much so that many regular viewers were sure I'd had another round of plastic surgery. I didn't, but it shows the impact that a flattering new haircut can have on your appearance. Rethinking your hairstyle is a great way to put your best foot forward into this next stage of your life.

Hair—Elsewhere

There's hair you want—the strands that frame your face, the ones you lovingly comb, curl, and condition—and then there's all the rest of them. These are the hairs that are popping up in all the wrong places, and you find new ones daily in places they never were before—guy places—cheeks, chin, upper lip, and neck.

This is yet another parting shot from menopause. As the ovaries shut down their production of female hormones, they keep making male hormones—so unfair. That tips our hormonal balance scale and gives those unwanted hairs the high sign to sprout. Have you started carrying tweezers and a tiny magnifying glass in your purse? Some women in our tribe have banded together in "whisker watches." If they spot a rogue hair on the chin of a friend, they pull her aside, knowing that if the situation was reversed, they'd do the same for her.

None of us wants to be the bearded lady. If your mustache area actually *has* a mustache, and if those unwelcome hairs seem to be coming in faster than you can pluck them out, it may be time to consider professional eradication. Although laser hair removal is not absolutely permanent, you will notice a decrease in unwanted facial hair after a series of sessions, usually a half dozen or so.

Ticktock—there's a practical reason to get it done sooner rather than later. Lasers work best when there is a pronounced color differential between hair and skin. For many women, the treatment will eliminate the dark hairs but not necessarily the ones that have started coming in white or gray. Common sense should tell you that if you're going gray on top, gray hairs on your chin are not far behind, so zap them while they're still dark, if you can. You can still get rid of unwanted white or gray hair through electrolysis, but that involves treating each one individually.

Holding Up the Girls

Mothers of the bride who won't spend money on a dress won't invest in a good bra, either, but if anybody in the whole world needs a good bra, it's a sixty-year-old woman. If you can't remember when you last bought a new bra, trust me, it's time. Actually, it's past time. Gravity is relentless. We're now at an age when we can see its toll every time we step into the shower, and I'm willing to bet that your bustline is a lot closer to your waistline than it used to be.

If your favorite lacy 36C is five years old, it probably doesn't fit you anymore, and even if it did when it was new, its elastic is waaay tired now. Trying on bras is never going to be your favorite sport, but don't take the lazy way out and order another online that's just like your old one. Go get properly fitted in person, but go in knowing that this is not a job for a well-meaning new hire at Victoria's Secret. Seek out an experienced saleswoman who is about your age. A new bra should lift your profile and provide support. Make sure it also addresses your personal figure concerns, including that roll of skin that tends to goosh out like uncooked biscuit dough under the arms and around in back.

Clothes

Some credit card ads raise the question, "What's in *your* wallet?" Forget about that—what's in your closet? How much of it fits you well? How much of it do you actually wear?

Some of us are sentimental about clothes we haven't worn in a while, or even about clothes we've never worn. These may be clothes from a prior phase of life or from a phase you aspire to but have yet to reach. I'm talking about that cute size 8 sundress you bought, hoping it would motivate you to diet your way into it. That was five years ago, and now it sits in the back of your closet and lurks, giving you guilt pangs daily.

Get over it. Get rid of it. It's time for some tough love for your wardrobe. Give yourself permission to write off the cost of that dress as the price of a lesson learned. Whatever you spent is a lot cheaper than what you're paying in remorse every time you look at it.

I purge my closet twice a year. I take out anything I haven't worn recently and everything that is torn or stained. Doesn't matter whether it's Armani or a super bargain I found on final sale. It's gone. You may not have to edit out the deadwood from your closet as often as I do, but if you can't remember the last time you wore a garment, it's a candidate for the donation bin. I also get rid of clothing that doesn't make me feel good when I'm in it—that black dress I was wearing when I face-planted never made it back into the closet at all.

Marie Kondo, the woman whose KonMari method is teaching the world to get organized, is right about clothes that "spark joy." It's the absolute essence of what we call the "bridal moment." In the salon, when I see a bride put on the right gown, I can tell immediately. Her shoulders go back; she tilts her head. She has a whole different air about her, knowing that she's wearing something that looks and feels good. It's the same with mothers of the bride. And it should be the same with you.

Dress with intention, with confidence, like you know you're worth it. You have to make a concerted effort to give yourself a closet with clothes that fit and make you feel good about yourself—a closet with nothing but good choices. That effort starts with editing out the white elephants—the lurker dress that doesn't fit you and never will, and that mauve suede jacket with the killer fringe that you wore to a Hootie & the Blowfish concert—in 1995. Or was it Reba McEntire? Tim McGraw?

That's the easy part. Having a functional closet also means trying on everything else, piece by piece, and taking a look at yourself in the mirror. Does it still look good? Does it fit well? Does it suit your style—and your lifestyle? Are you proud of yourself when you wear it? If not, it's out.

Once you've rid yourself of the undesirables, figure out what's missing. A trench coat? A great pair of black pants? Many of us tend to buy the same kinds of clothes over and over, which is how we end up with fifteen white blouses, a closet full to overflowing, and nothing to wear. Think about what events you attend regularly. Work? Football or basketball games? Live theatre or concerts? Cocktail parties? The ever-dangerous "dressy casual" get-together? Which events give you the most problems as you're getting ready to go? Make a point of adding items to your wardrobe that make dressing for those occasions easier. Think seasonally as well. You may find that getting dressed for a June wedding is no problem, but you have nothing that would look right at a Christmas party—or vice versa.

Whether you're shopping in person or online, try on what you buy before giving it permission to move in and take up precious hanger space in your closet. The tunic that caught your eye in the catalog may look a lot less flattering on you than it did on the model—a twenty-something gazelle who's eight inches taller than you are—but even mail-order clothing is returnable. Don't keep clothes because you're trying to avoid that dreaded trip to the post office. Again, it's a case of making the effort.

For my own wardrobe, I tend to gravitate toward a handful of labels. They're not all high-end designers, but their clothes fit me well and suit my personality. I encourage you to do the same. Figure out what looks good on you, and then get in the habit of picking up a new piece or two every few months—when the seasons change.

When I say a brand of clothing fits me, I don't mean that everything fits perfectly the first time I try it on. Everyone has figure flaws—very few of us are ever an ideal size 4, or 14, and exactly none of us stays that way forever. I battle lymphedema, a condition that makes my upper arms swell up. I also have a sizable derriere that is, if you'll pardon the double entendre, the butt of jokes made by friends. (This means you, Monte.)

No amount of exercise is going to change either my arms or my backside, so I embrace them both as part of who I am. I dress around them, with the understanding that whatever I buy will have to be altered. Whether you have a large rear, love handles, a muffin top, broad shoulders, or thunder thighs, learn to look for styles that minimize your problem areas and play up your assets. Once you've made a purchase, get it tailored to your height and shape. Whatever it is, it's going to look better—and more expensive—if it fits you.

Except clamdiggers or capri pants. Clamdiggers don't look good on anyone. They draw attention to the least attractive part of your lower extremities—and is that really where you want people to be looking? Slender women seem to be walking on toothpicks—spindly little birdie legs. The rest of us look like we've been issued cankles that would look better on a Steinway baby grand. Clamdiggers also make your butt look as big as a Buick, whether or not you have a lot of junk in the trunk. They're the worst pant ever invented for the female body.

Cold shoulders are another pet peeve of mine. Blouses and tops with tiny peekaboo cutouts at the shoulder are gimmicky and not flattering. They're also very trendy right now, which means they're going to be passé real soon.

Stay away from shapeless tops that hang straight down from the bust. This boho trend looks decent enough if you're seventeen and slender, but now it's just going to make strangers wonder whether you're pregnant. Remember that there's a waist in there that looks better when it's defined.

And then there are spaghetti straps. Unless you have arms exactly like Madonna's or Michelle Obama's, you have no business in spaghetti straps. That leaves out 99 percent of us (including me), so unless those straps are attached to a swimsuit (and even if they are, you have better choices), do your self-esteem a favor and put that strappy top back on the rack, please.

Let's talk animal prints. I love animal prints and snakeskin patterns, but a little goes a long way. Unless you want to be mistaken for a leopard or a giraffe or a zebra or a cobra, head-to-toe is out. The same is true for those hyper-bright look-at-me hues that you see in the fashion magazines—electric orange, superhot pink, radioactive chartreuse. If you're wearing a whole outfit in one of those colors, people are indeed looking at you, but for all the wrong reasons. For accessories, though, they're terrific, as long as you don't overdo it— one fun accent per outfit, please.

I particularly like wearing shoes with a pop of color or an animal print, but shoes could be an entire chapter all by themselves. I have so much to say about them that we'd just need to sit down over a cup of coffee and talk about it. As someone who stands on hardwood floors for eight hours daily while filming and helping brides, I totally get it about the need for comfort and about the need to take care of your feet. So say yes to pedicures and no to shoes that cramp your toes—but also say no to shoes that cramp your style.

Shoes can make you look thirty-five—or ninety-five. And some of us have gotten just plain lazy about footwear. You don't have to teeter on four-inch Manolos when you're making a quick run to the grocery store, but unless you've got real medical problems with your feet, stay away from shoes that look, um, remedially orthopedic—like you got them on orders from your podiatrist. There's a wide range of choice in between one and the other—and no, Crocs are not in that range. Look for shoes that are comfortable and stylish, and that flatter your legs.

One more pointer that I have for you girls comes from Grandmother Baird—you met her at the beginning of the chapter, getting all dressed up to go to church. She firmly believed that you were never fully dressed until you had your earrings on. Just sayin'.

I believe that the older we get, the more classic our look should be. Classic does not mean frumpy or dowdy. Avoiding of-the-moment styles like the cold shoulder does not mean dressing like your great-aunt Bertha. It means seeking out timeless clothing that will still look attractive years from now.

Take your cue from some of our best-dressed movie heroines and first ladies. There's a reason why Monte swoons over Jackie O, Grace Kelly, and Audrey Hepburn. Even in photos that are decades old, they appear chic and elegant. They also look surprisingly contemporary—many of their outfits would still be wearable on the street today.

The epitome of this concept is the little black dress, pearls, and stilettos. If it was good enough for Grace and Audrey and Jackie, it's surely good enough for all of us now. If that dress isn't in your closet, buy one. Spend some money on it, and a jacket and black pumps to go with it. Then have it tailored so it fits you perfectly. It will become your go-to outfit—from weddings to funerals, you'll find that you'll be able to wear it anywhere. Change it up with jewelry and accessories, and no one will know it's the same ensemble. You'll feel confident wearing it, and that alone means you'll get your money's worth many times over.

Self-care is the new black, but it's not about creating a "new you." Self-care is about rediscovering your best self and reintroducing her to the world. Think of that elegant new black outfit as your calling card, as proof positive that you respect and value yourself going into this next phase of life.

WHAT'S NEXT
Girlfriends' Guide

- **Make Self-Care Normal**

  Self-care isn't something you *do*. It's a collection of habits that become routine. In short, it's a lifestyle. The day to embrace your new lifestyle is today!

- **Go with Fewer Clothes, Better Clothes**

  If the clothes you're weeding out of your closet—and you *are* weeding out your wardrobe, aren't you?—are primarily inexpensive, faddish pieces whose time has come and gone, rethink how you shop. Don't dress too young or too old. As you enter this next chapter of your life, refine a look for yourself that is both classic and stylish. Add accent pieces, such as animal prints and neon brights that are hip and trendy, but segue into quality pieces that will become mainstays of your wardrobe.

- **Think Like a Bride**

  Many young women come into the salon looking for the hottest new fashion, and frankly, that's not always a good idea. I encourage each bride to choose a dress that reflects her own personality, but I also advise her to think beyond the wedding itself. The day she's a bride will come and go in what seems like a nanosecond, but the photos from her wedding are going to be around for a long time—and today's trend is tomorrow's costume. (Poodle skirts, enormous shoulder pads, and go-go boots come to mind.)

Kate Middleton married Prince William in 2011, and there's a reason why she took the inspiration for her wedding gown from Grace Kelly, who married Prince Rainier of Monaco more than fifty years earlier—it was a classic, timeless look. As the anniversaries roll by and you show your wedding album to your children and grandchildren, you don't want them pointing at your gown and laughing. After forty years my own wedding gown still looks pretty good, but I do regret the dresses I chose for my bridesmaids—in Big Bird yellow.

Apply the same principle to your daily wardrobe. Fast-forward ten years from now and imagine seeing yourself in a photograph taken this morning. Will you be able to look at what you're wearing in that photo without cringing? Fashions change, but style is forever.

▪ Know What You Look Like Before You Leave Home

Have you ever been horrified when you caught sight of your reflection in the rearview mirror of your car or in a store mirror while you were out shopping? You thought you looked fine when you left the house, but now you can see that your blush is clownish and blotchy, and the hem on those pants drags the ground. I suggest purchasing two mirrors: a magnifying makeup mirror that mimics natural light and a full-length mirror—preferably a three-way—to check your clothing.

▪ Make the Effort

You will notice that I've said "make the effort" several times in this chapter. What does that mean? It means getting your hair cut on a regular basis, every six to eight weeks. It means not leaving the house in sweatpants unless you're actually planning to sweat. It means not wearing shower shoes—unless you're still wet and reaching for a towel. It means making an adjustment in your priorities. It means consciously devoting more time and money to yourself than you have been and planning accordingly.

- **Value Yourself**

If you've let yourself go, it's time to take yourself back. Reclaim that pride in your appearance that slipped away while you were raising your kids. You may still have obligations to take care of grandchildren, adult dependents, or aging parents, but you can't pour from an empty cup. As they say during those flight safety announcements right before takeoff, put your own oxygen mask on first. Be proud. Be sassy. Be strong. And, in the end, you'll be happy.

3

One in Eight

*B*reast cancer strikes one in eight women—that's 12 percent of us.[1] In 2012 I became one of them. That year I didn't want to go in for my mammogram—not that I ever looked forward to it. Even if you're as well-endowed as Dolly Parton, it hurts to have your boob flattened into a panini under glass, but when you're pushin' a B cup, getting smushed that way is like something from the depths of Hades.

Northside Breast Care Center kept sending me these yellow reminder cards to make an appointment, but I tossed them all. At the time, I didn't have a minute to spare in my schedule. I was filming both the bridal show and the bridesmaids show. I had a brand-new grandbaby I wanted to play with. And of course, the shop wasn't going to run itself. Since there were no lumps that I could feel, I figured I could skip the mammogram just this once. But Northside was relentless. They started nagging me by phone.

Eventually they wore me down—I realized that it was gonna be easier for me to go in for the mammogram than to keep making excuses or ducking their calls.

When I got there, the receptionist asked whether I wanted their new 3D imaging. It was the latest technology, she said, but it would cost $200 extra. I went for it.

I'm alive because of that $200—a regular mammogram never would have picked up my cancer that soon. Left undetected for another year, it would have spread to my lymph nodes, and I'd have been up the proverbial brown creek with not a paddle in sight.

I should have known something was up when my appointment took longer than usual. I thought I was done when the mammographer stepped out of the room, but she came back in to take more shots—twice. She kept moving me around, telling me to turn this way, turn that way. At the time, rather than being concerned, I was exasperated. I figured the 3D equipment was new to her, too, and that she just wasn't skilled enough to get clear images. *My God, woman*, I thought, *do you not know what you're doing?* Looking back, I can see that I mistook thoroughness for incompetence. I'm pretty sure that lady knew I had breast cancer.

The appointment ended the way they all do—nobody tells you anything on the spot; you get a call in a day or two. And sure enough, they told me I had to come back in for a biopsy, but even so, I still wasn't nervous.

The Diagnosis

When I went back to Northside, they strapped me onto a table and began tilting and turning me eight ways from Sunday, including upside down. They had the hardest time getting a core biopsy, and it hurt like crazy. The tech asked me to rate my discomfort on a scale of 1 to 10, and I told her it was a 9.

"You shouldn't be in that kind of pain," she said. That should have been another clue, but as soon as I walked out of the clinic, I put it out of my mind. If I barely had time for a mammogram, I sure as heck didn't have time to have cancer. Besides, we already had someone in the family who had cancer—my husband.

They'd found Eddie's cancer on a fluke, when his stomach had inverted inside his body. After he underwent emergency surgery to flip it back around, his surgeon, Dr. Iqbal Garcha, told us that a pre-op CT scan had picked up an abnormal growth on his small intestine. After more tests, Dr. Garcha decided to open Eddie back up and remove the section of intestine where the tumor was. His surgery was scheduled for April 13, 2012. And yes, it was Friday the thirteenth.

I found out I had breast cancer at 7:05 that morning. Right before Eddie and I left for Northside Hospital for his surgery, I was sitting in the den when my phone rang. The screen ID read: Dr. John Moore.

All the blood drained from my face, and I started shaking so badly my hand could barely hold the phone. John Moore had been my friend for twenty-eight years, but he was also my ob-gyn. There was no good reason why he'd be calling me at that hour. After my biopsy, I hadn't given the possibility of breast cancer another thought, but I knew right away what that phone call meant.

"I have really bad news," Dr. Moore said. His voice was trembling, which was unlike him, and I could tell he was choked up. "Lori, you've got breast cancer. You must see a surgeon immediately."

I felt like that brightly colored top I used to play with as a little girl. It was the old-fashioned metal kind, with a spiral rod down the middle—just push down to make it spin. And boy, was I spinning.

"John," I said, "I'm on the way to the hospital with Eddie, who's got intestinal cancer. He's having surgery today."

He immediately apologized for calling at what was probably the worst possible time. "Call me this weekend if you need me," he continued. "I suggest Dr. Garcha as your surgeon."

"That's who's operating on Eddie this morning."

As shaken as I was, I tried to put on a brave face and get myself together. I had no intention of saying anything to Eddie until he was out of surgery, but as soon as I hung up with Dr. Moore, I started sobbing and blurted it out. Then we cried together.

I called Mollie, who was about to head for Northside to wait with me during her dad's operation. Knowing how much pain and worry she was already carrying because of her father, telling her felt like I was dealing her a physical blow, and I think she felt the same way receiving the news.

I also gave Mollie one job that I couldn't bear to do. I asked her to call Cory, her brother, and tell him about my cancer. Emotionally, I was a mess. It had taken all I had to tell my daughter and my husband—I just couldn't bring myself to tell my son.

When Eddie and I got to the hospital, I told Dr. Garcha about the call from Dr. Moore, and he promised to talk with me as soon as he was finished in the OR. While Eddie was being prepped, I called Monte. When I reached him, he was on a plane for New York. "You know I love you," he said as he began to cry. "You're going to be fine. You'll get through this." There were long periods during that phone call when both of us were too overwhelmed to speak, and that silence was absolutely deafening.

Then I called my parents. They were out for breakfast at a little restaurant called Egg Harbor Café, just down the street from us, and when I told them, they were so upset they couldn't finish their meal.

As they were leaving, my mom looked over her shoulder and saw that they'd been sitting in booth 13—this is the kind of stuff you remember when you get bad news. To this day, despite visiting the same café weekly, she refuses to sit in that booth.

At that point, my entire family was in overload. Telling them about my cancer was one of the hardest things I've ever had to do. Nobody meant for all of this to happen on the same day as Eddie's operation, but it did.

Dr. Garcha came out to the waiting room after the surgery. All had gone well with the operation, and he was optimistic that Eddie wouldn't need chemotherapy. "Now let's talk about you," he said. He sat with me for about forty minutes and set up an office visit for the very next day.

Notepad, Nachos, and TV

My mom and my daughter both came with me. Mollie, who's a Virgo and always very organized, brought a notepad and colored highlighters. She'd been doing tons of research and was asking a million questions. I was thankful for her assertiveness because I was completely zoned out. The only thing I remember is staring straight up and thinking, *That is not nice ceiling tile. Dr. Garcha should get that replaced.*

I still could not get my head around the idea that I had cancer—actually, cancers plural. I had two kinds. One was ductal carcinoma in situ, which is relatively common. The other was infiltrating lobular carcinoma, which is rarer and more aggressive. Both of them were growing fast—I'd had a clean mammogram only twelve months earlier.

The appointment with Dr. Garcha was intense. After that much bad news, Mollie and I were in need of adult beverages. She took me to Frontera Mex-Mex Grill, and over nachos and margaritas she said, "Mom, I've been thinking. You need to turn this into something positive. I think you should film your battle against cancer."

I took a big swallow of margarita and shook my head as the brain freeze set in. "I'm not doing that, Mollie," I said. "I get enough of myself on camera as it is."

Mollie wouldn't let it go—she inherited my bossy genes, for sure. "There are so many women your age who watch the show," she insisted, "mothers of the bride, godmoms, aunts, and grandmas— and everyone knows someone who has been affected by breast cancer. Think about doing something that would raise awareness and give comfort to others."

As soon as she put it that way, I knew it was the right thing to do. I called Jen Holbach, our executive producer at North South Productions. I've known her since *Say Yes to the Dress: Atlanta* first went on the air. I told her I had breast cancer and offered to do an episode on it.

She didn't hesitate at all. "That's a great idea," she said. "Just let me check with TLC."

Jen called back within minutes. "TLC is so enthusiastic about this," she said. "They want to do a one-hour special."

We started filming three days later, beginning with me breaking the news to everyone at Bridals by Lori. Telling Robin, Flo, Megan, and the rest of the staff about my diagnosis was gut-wrenching for all of us. These women are my chosen family, and I look forward to seeing them every morning. I asked Monte and Robin to run things in my absence. They were going to have to be me while I was gone, and I didn't know how long that would be. I was leaving the fate of the shop—and my livelihood—in their hands.

One Lump or Two

Next up was an MRI. The core biopsy, awful as it was, was a day at the beach in comparison. They placed me lying faceup on this narrow stainless-steel slab. It was cold and hard, and I felt like a corpse laid out in a morgue. All I needed was a toe tag.

Once the techs had arranged my arms over my head, they rolled me and the slab into this tight, dark machine. It was as claustrophobic as a casket, and the pain was something awful—my arms were killing me. I started feeling sorry for myself, and then I got scared. I let scared get into my head, which meant that upbeat Lori, the one who's always so positive, took a powder and disappeared. I don't know what happened to her, but she was gone.

The music piped in through the headphones was supposed to relax me, but it had the opposite effect. I was forced to listen to Garth Brooks twanging, "I got friends in low places," and it put me over the edge. Worse yet, only one side of the headphones was working, and the song selection was on auto repeat. "Friends in Low Places" played over and over for most of the time I was in there, but only in my right ear. Somebody finally must have figured out it was stuck because it was replaced by insipid spa music—better, but not much. None of it was loud enough to drown out the din of the machine itself. The pounding was deafening. It was as if some bozo was whomping on the biggest bass drum in the University of Georgia Redcoat marching band—with a tree stump—and me inside the drum. I was in that coffin for an hour, and I cried the whole time.

When Dr. Garcha told me the results, it turned out that not only did I have cancer in my right breast, but I had a bunch of atypical cells in my left breast as well. I had a double whammy fixin' to happen. The question was what to do about it, and that set off our own version of *Family Feud*.

Everybody weighed in. My dad did not want me to get a mastectomy, and he was adamant about it. I think he hurt for me, for his child, and didn't want me to suffer through that. Eddie took his side of the argument, and for the same reason—to spare me from pain. Mollie advocated strongly for a double mastectomy, which meant that when I decided to get a lumpectomy instead, she got miffed, and then some. She'd spent hours on the Internet researching the pros and cons of lumpectomy versus mastectomy, and now her best advice was being ignored. Worse yet, she was sure I was rolling the dice with my life.

I had a two-hour lumpectomy in early May. At the same time, Dr. Garcha removed a lymph node from my armpit and sent it to the lab. A lymph node is the canary in the coal mine—if it's cancerous, there's a much higher chance that the cancer has spread. If that had already happened, I'd have been in for a much bigger fight, and with much lower odds of winning it.

My node was cancer-free, but that didn't lift my spirits. I became increasingly gloomy. Optimistic Lori was still AWOL, replaced by an irritable, melancholy shrew who stayed in bed and slept a lot. Not only did I feel ugly and depressed, but I felt really vulnerable, and I was incensed about it. They say that angry is sad's bodyguard, and those were my two live-in companions.

At my follow-up appointment with Dr. Garcha, the reason why I was so bummed out was right there on a piece of black-and-white film. He put up the scan so I could see it, then gave me the bad news. "For a lumpectomy to work," he said, "we have to get the whole cancer out—which we did—but we also have to see normal breast tissue cells all around what was removed, what are called clear margins. Lori, your margins are not clear."

I looked at him blankly. It was one of those rare times when I had nothing to say. "We can't have that," Dr. Garcha continued matter-of-factly. "The pathologist saw some abnormal-looking cells. To make things even more complicated, there are atypical cells in your left breast as well. All these abnormal cells in both breasts make me very nervous. There's a good chance they can turn cancerous."

I had another spinning-top moment, almost as bad as when I got the original call from Dr. Moore. I couldn't tell if I was turning circles or if the room was whirling around me. Either way, I was dizzy, almost nauseated with fear. The idea that my boobs were trying to kill me ran laps around my brain, then pitched a tent and camped out in the middle of my forehead.

"What do we do now?" I asked.

"We don't absolutely have to do a mastectomy," he replied, "but at a minimum, you'll need another surgery. I can't guarantee that I'll get everything with just one more operation, and there would still be radiation to follow. After that, you'll be closely monitored. If we ever see abnormal cells on one of your mammograms, you'll have to get another core biopsy to make sure they're not cancerous."

No way. Not this girl. What Dr. Garcha was describing was a different kind of death sentence—perpetual anxiety. As scary as it was to think about having my breasts removed, watchful waiting was a lot worse, praying after each mammogram, knowing that the possibility of mastectomy would be hanging over me for the rest of my days.

"I'm not doing that," I told him. "My chest is already looking weird. Take 'em both. Let's do the double mastectomy."

The Decision

I've always had lumpy breasts. They'd found a couple of small lumps—little nodule things—back when I was sixteen, and they took them out. At the time, I told myself that if I ever got cancer, I was gonna cut 'em off. They're just fatty tissue, after all—no big deal, right?

I'm not sure why I thought that way, but part of it may be because I grew up hearing about Aunt Dorothy. My family always said I was the spitting image of her, and Aunt Dorothy died of breast cancer. She was fairly young, in her midfifties. She'd been afraid to go to the doctor, so by the time she went, the cancer had spread and there was nothing they could do for her. Even so, everyone told me not to worry about it because she was on my father's side. At the time, we were told that if you had a hereditary predisposition to breast cancer, you'd get it from your mom. Of course, now they're finding out that those nasty genes can come from either parent.

In hindsight, Dr. Garcha may have believed all along that, medically, a double mastectomy was the right call, but he also knew that it was not his decision to make. And now, when I speak to women about breast cancer, I talk about that a lot. If you've got breast cancer, the choices to be made are yours and yours alone. Lumpectomy or mastectomy. I can't tell you what to do, and neither can your doctor. Arm yourself with the best advice and as much information as you can, but in the end, it's your body, and you have to figure out your own path.

I chose radical double mastectomy, knowing it would be a tough surgery and a long recovery, but Dr. Garcha told me that, with my breasts gone, my risk of getting cancer again was pretty much zero, or very close to it. That was what I wanted—to be done with cancer. Permanently. I wanted my life back.

With that decision made, I had to find a plastic surgeon. I talked to one guy who had a great reputation, but he struck me as insensitive and more than a little too full of himself. I chose Dr. Diane Alexander instead. Diane is a breast reconstruction specialist. With her confident voice, rectangular eyeglasses, and Carole King head of curly hair, she exuded quiet competence without coming across as arrogant. She was empathetic and understood not just the operation itself but the implications of it from a woman's point of view.

No matter what kind of reconstructive surgery you get, it means taking a part of your body from where it used to be, moving it to your chest, and making a boob out of it. It could come from your thigh, your abdomen, your back, or even your rear end. I was completely comfortable with Dr. Alexander, but there was still something Frankenstein about it all. Each surgical possibility sounded bizarre in its own way, and choosing among them was a momentous decision.

I remember sitting in that pastel blue plaid hospital gown in the exam room. My mother was with me, and I started to cry. More than two months had passed since my diagnosis, and it all still felt like it was happening to somebody else. I felt like my body had betrayed me. Something evil was growing inside me, something I couldn't control, and I did not like feeling helpless. I was mad at cancer. I was mad at everything.

As Dr. Alexander described the options to me, I kept hoping that someone would tell me what to do, but just like choosing between lumpectomy and mastectomy, it was up to me to make the decision that was right for me. In my case, I opted for the latissimus dorsi flap. She would take muscles from my upper back, just under the shoulder near the armpit, and pull them around to the front. My implants would be placed under those newly relocated muscles.

My surgery took place over the Fourth of July holiday. By that time, a sense of calm had come over me. Some of it might have been the pre-op pharmaceuticals, but I'd also made peace with the prospect of losing my breasts. They had cancer in them, and I wanted them gone. I was ready.

Still, one of the weirdest sensations I've ever felt was when Dr. Alexander took out her purple magic marker and began drawing on me. "I'm going to put the scars so they're right in your bra line," she said as she was making these long swooping curves on my back. "We'll do the lats first, then the mastectomy. That way we only have to flip you over once." After prayers and kisses from Eddie, Mollie, and Cory, the last thing I remember is being wheeled down the hall and through a door marked OR 3.

Mollie was with me when I woke up. I was still pretty much out of it, so I wasn't nearly as horrified as she was when the nurses unwrapped the bandages to check the incisions—so many cuts, so many stitches, so much blood. Breasts are the universal symbol for the loving, nurturing connection between mother and child, and mine were gone. For Mollie, the fact that she had just given birth herself probably made it worse.

As the pain meds began to wear off, I started ordering her around, at least she says I did. I was still in what they call the fog of anesthesia. I was desperate for cran-apple juice, which Mollie had to mix herself out of cranberry and apple juices because the hospital didn't have any, and I was being such a relentless pain in the butt about it. I'm surprised I didn't make her change out the ceiling tiles.

The next morning, the nurses wanted me on my feet. Mollie, who'd spent the night in my room, got me out of bed. She tried to walk me to the bathroom so I could pee and brush my teeth, but I wasn't interested in her help. Mothers are supposed to help their daughters, not the other way around—this was a role reversal I wasn't ready to accept. "I got it. I got it. I can do this," I insisted. I was so sure I didn't need her to hold me up—until I collapsed in her arms and passed out. I'm sure I scared the crap out of her.

I was in the hospital for six days—Cory, Mollie, and Eddie took turns being there with me. I needed a couple of days at home before I could work up the courage to look at my body in the mirror, and when I finally did, it was gross. I guess by then it wasn't as gory as what Mollie had seen in the hospital, but I still looked like I'd been on the losing end of a knife fight with a butcher.

I was upset, but I was also relieved because the cancer was finally out of me. Besides, there were other things to be horrified about. I left the hospital with drains, which were put in to prevent bodily fluids from pooling at the incision sites. I understood their purpose, but darn, I hated those things! Each one looked like flex tubing with a turkey baster at the end. There were eight of them, and they dangled in front of my body down to my navel. I had to wear this undershirt—they tried to call it a camisole, but I was not fooled. It was an undershirt, and it was super ugly. On the inside, it had safety pins and what looked like garter belt snaps to secure the dangling turkey basters so they didn't get crossed up with each other or snag on my clothes. They were so uncomfortable that it was impossible to sleep.

The drains had to be emptied regularly, and Eddie was my drainer. He was still recovering from his own major operation, but as my nurse, he was incredibly caring and attentive. He emptied out the fluid, gunk, and junk that came out of those turkey basters three times a day—that's got to be one definition of true love.

I was so grateful when Dr. Alexander said the drains could come out. The other good news she gave me was from Dr. Garcha's office—my pathology reports were clear. Now all I had to do was recover.

Recuperation

At this point I had no idea how hard getting back to anything resembling normal was going to be—which probably was no accident. I think maybe surgeons don't tell you everything beforehand because it's hard enough getting you to be brave enough to face the operation itself. To tell the truth, once you've had the mastectomy, you're not even halfway home.

I had regular visits with my oncologist, Dr. Colleen Austin, and her waiting room was a sobering reminder of how much worse it could have been for me. Sitting there, I was unnerved, even frightened by seeing what cancer could do to the human body. There were technicolor people with red skin, large purple bruises, and yellow fingernails; people with bald heads, bloated bodies, and no eyebrows; and faceless people wearing hats, sunglasses, and white masks because they were light sensitive and susceptible to every germ in the air. I was taken aback by what they looked like, but my heart went out to each of them—they were so sick, not just from cancer, but from the potent, often toxic treatments that offered them their only chance at survival.

I didn't need chemo or radiation, but Dr. Austin did put me on a drug specifically for breast cancer patients. It stops cancer cells by denying them estrogen, which starves the tumors of the hormones they need to grow. I knew that it was preventing a recurrence, but the side effects were rough.

For starters, I couldn't put my feet down flat. Getting up in the middle of the night—*all* women my age get up in the middle of the night—I had to hobble on my heels to get to the bathroom. Every joint in my body ached—my ankles, my hips, my shoulders. I felt like I was a zillion years old.

Then there were the hot flashes that felt like firecrackers on the

Fourth of July. It was the second coming of menopause, with a vengeance. I was sweating through as many as four shirts a night. You'll sometimes hear women describe hot flashes as their inner child playing with matches. Mine was armed with napalm and a flamethrower.

Not having my boobs was degrading enough, but I looked awful and felt about the same. I puffed up like a blowfish. My skin was like parchment, and my hair was falling out in clumps. I had enormous black circles under my eyes. For *Say Yes* shoots, I was wearing about eighteen pounds of foundation and concealer spackled onto my face, but believe me, there's no makeup that can hide sick.

The Cold, Hard Facts

Looking and feeling the way you do after a mastectomy, you could really have yourself a good old pity party if you allowed it—and sometimes, I did. Through it all, though, I was lifted up by the love of friends and family. I got a card from Monte every day. Some were heartfelt, some were funny—get out of bed and get your big ole rear end back to work—but I could always count on that card. When I was at my lowest, the arrival of that card was often the best thing that happened to me.

There were also times when I was lifted up by complete strangers in a way I never could have imagined. Six months after my surgery, I got my nipples tattooed. Long ago I'd sworn I'd never, ever get a tattoo, but breast cancer changed all that, just like it changes a lot of things. Dr. Alexander had been able to create a nipple of sorts, or at least the suggestion of a nipple-in-waiting, but it was the same shade as the rest of my skin. My chest was essentially a blank canvas—the only way to have anything that looked like the real thing was to get it inked in on top. The good news, such as it was, is that I got to pick out the color.

Julie Anthony is an Atlanta-based tattoo professional who works with breast cancer survivors. She was so calm and reassuring—she asked me if I wanted to take a pain pill or something for nervousness while she worked. "Give me whatever you've got," I said. Just the thought of what she'd be doing made me anxious, but after she was finished, I was surprised at how much better I felt.

I'm in the bridal business, which is all about helping a woman look her best on one of the most important days of her life. That means I'm also in the self-esteem business. In the salon we see brides with body issues all the time. Getting them into a gown they love and loving themselves in it—that bridal moment—that's what I live for. In the same way, getting tattooed was an important step for me on the road back to self-acceptance and self-love. It wasn't until I got my tattoos that I could bear to look at my chest in the mirror. Those mounds on my rib cage finally looked like boobs.

Maybe they look like boobs, but they sure don't feel like 'em. They're as hard as Barbie boobs, and they don't move at all. If I collide with Monte while we're filming, he complains that they've shattered his elbow. Even all these years later, I still think of them as something I'm wearing, not as part of me. To me they're medieval body armor—a breastplate, not breasts.

And they're cold, but the only way I know they're cold is by touching them with my fingers. I have no feeling from my collarbone to the bottom of my rib cage. Being numb over that large an area takes some getting used to, and it can be awkward. The first time I was introduced to Becca, who would eventually become my daughter-in-law, I also met her mother and her cousins—beautiful women, and very put together. I'd had my surgery not long before, and I was trying so hard to make a good impression. I was wearing a halter top that covered the scars on my back, and it was my first outing in a strapless bra.

We'd had dinner together, and while we were having dessert, my arm brushed against my midsection. I was horrified. *I'm getting soooo fat!* I thought to myself, instantly regretting that piece of chocolate cake I'd been enjoying. When I finally looked down, I saw this rumply lump under my halter top. The strapless bra had slipped down and bunched up around my waist. Because I'm numb in front, I didn't feel it while it was happening. I excused myself, sidled out of my chair, and headed for the ladies' room, praying with every step that it didn't end up around my ankles.

There were other aftereffects as well. My latissimus dorsi were now on my chest, and without them I had limited range of motion and zero upper body strength. Anything above shoulder height was out of reach—I couldn't get a glass out of the cupboard. I couldn't stand up straight. My shoulders were hunched in, and I walked around like a wounded bird. I just couldn't move, and that scared me.

Dr. Alexander referred me for physical therapy to a place called TurningPoint, a rehab center for mastectomy patients. The woman who runs it is herself a breast cancer survivor, as is everyone who works there. You get PT, but you also get deep tissue massages—and women who talk to you as they're working. They tell you their stories and assure you that you will get through this. Many a tear is shed on that massage table, but the empowerment you get is a real lifesaver. That healing touch made all the difference for me.

What's Next After Cancer

For as long as you're fighting cancer and recuperating from surgery, that's your job, and it just consumes you. What happens when that job is over?

What happens is that you struggle, but in a totally different way. After I completed my physical therapy and "graduated" from TurningPoint, the strangest feeling came over me. I'd been a professional patient for so long that when my course of treatment was finished, I felt a little lost. I'd been so focused on "getting through it" that I hadn't given any consideration to the next part of my life. *Is that all?* I thought. *Am I done? What happens next?*

Answering that question led me back into the salon, but it also led me forward. It led me into a new calling, into greater involvement in the fight against breast cancer. I've received so many letters from women who were motivated to get their mammograms because I spoke out about my experience. Some of them got the same bad news I did, but they're getting treatment and are on the road to recovery.

Cancer changes you. I don't sweat the small stuff nearly as much anymore—and after breast cancer, a whole lot more looks like small stuff than it used to. Including my scars. I've now passed my eight-year anniversary, and my relationship with them has evolved. As repelled by them as I was at first, when I see them today, I'm proud. I think of them as battle scars—proof of survival, proof that life goes on.

My fight against cancer led me into a new perspective. I began looking ahead more actively—looking toward my own life to come, and what I want it to be. My diagnosis was the shot across the bow from mortality—the first stark reminder that I wasn't going to live forever.

There's a folded piece of paper I still keep in my purse. It's a report from Northside Hospital, listing out the kinds of cancers I had and the survival odds for each of them. Even though it's dog-eared, even if I change purses, I always have it with me. I think of it as a way to keep looking forward, but at the same time, it's also a way not to forget where I've been and how far I've come. I'm grateful every day to be alive. Now I get up in the morning, look out the window, and say, "Thank God I'm here."

WHAT'S NEXT
Girlfriends' Guide

- **Don't Put Yourself on the Back Burner**

  I learned a lot from my cancer experience, not just about the disease itself but about life and how to deal with the curveballs it throws at you. Take care of your health. Soccer practice is not more important than a mammogram. Cleaning your closets matters less—a lot less—than getting your teeth cleaned or getting to the gym. If you take away one thing from my experience, call to schedule your mammogram right now.

- **Stubborn Is Not a Good Look for You**

  Being strong and being headstrong are two differnt things. As independent and self-sufficient as you may be, learn to receive help when you need it—otherwise, when you pass out on the way to the bathroom, no one is there to catch you on the way down.

- **Emotional Comfort Is Part of Recovery**

  Everyone deserves grace—including you. If you feel bad and someone is giving you crap, you don't have to accept it. And by the way, stop giving it to yourself. You never know what someone is going through. Be kind, extend grace—and receive grace as well.

- **Bring Backup**

  Any major medical issue can be scary, and when you're afraid, you stop thinking. Bring someone with you to your appointments, someone who will listen and ask questions on your behalf.

- **Take Time to Be Sure**

   Some medical choices have big implications. Unless you're in immediate physical danger, resist the temptation to make a life-changing decision while you're overwhelmed. Do your research, talk to friends and family, and get a second opinion if you need one. In the end, though, it's your body, and you must choose your own path.

- **Hang On to Your Resilience**

   Above all, if you're facing a serious medical issue, don't give up on yourself. Whatever is wrong with your body, you're still you. Keep doing whatever it is that makes you feel beautiful and valuable, inside and out, because you are.

4

PMS: The Good Kind, Y'all

(Physical, Mental, and Spiritual Health)

To me, wellness is health—simply put, it means you feel good. Throughout my twenties, thirties, and even my forties, I took being healthy as a given. I was running myself ragged, but I was blessed enough to feel pretty good while juggling two full-time jobs—building Bridals by Lori and raising Mollie and Cory. The occasional Jane Fonda workout video and fat-free snacks (the diet fad du jour) kept me balanced in the midst of our hectic life. While my kids were napping, I remember putting on my most stylish (ha!) striped leotard, tights, and leg warmers (I know, I know), pulling out some Campbell's tomato soup cans for weights, and trying to follow along with the video while perched on a scrap piece of carpet—my exercise mat—in the living room. Oh, and I can't forget the lavender sweatband

and elastic belt! (I'm eternally grateful that no photos of me in that getup survive.)

In the last two decades, we've learned so much more about what our bodies need to stay healthy and avoid disease. My breast cancer diagnosis brought home the importance of good health, and just in case I was starting to forget, my fall in the shop really hammered home the lesson.

That said, none of us should need a health crisis as a wake-up call. As we age, good health is of the utmost importance, and unlike when we were younger, it's no longer something we can afford to take for granted. It's key to truly embracing *What's Next* and living out this next chapter to the absolute fullest with no regrets.

Good health is a three-pronged journey that encompasses physical health, mental health, and spiritual health, and a powerful synergy exists among them. Each affects the other two, one way or another. And I say "journey" deliberately because it truly is just that—a journey.

There is never a final destination. When it comes to good health, you're always on the road—but whether that road is smooth or bumpy is up to you. Each day, we all must wake up and make the proactive decision to love ourselves by making healthy choices. Those choices are the series of steps we take on our journey. For me, it means waking up and taking the time to play with puppy Chloe, drinking my coffee while reading a devotional, and exercising before getting ready for work.

Your decisions might look drastically different, and that's not only okay, it's what I would hope for—your journey is your own. Whatever phase of your health journey you're in, you can do better. We all can.

In this chapter we'll talk about a few of the most common health issues facing women our age and how to prepare our bodies for a healthy future, but first things first: although we're all members of the same tribe, each of us has different health-care needs. My thoughts here are not meant to be comprehensive, nor are they intended to supplant advice from your health-care provider—there's no substitute for regular visits with your doctor.

Regular visits.

Crickets.

When your kids were little, you were diligent about taking them for their checkups and shots and getting the pediatrician to prescribe something for strep throat or asthma or whatever nasty stomach bug was going around that year. But for yourself—your annual mammogram or a colonoscopy or a bone density scan, a flu shot, or that new shingles vaccine that will prevent *so* much misery—these are the kinds of appointments that some of us never quite get around to making.

You take care of your car—you know enough to change the oil, check the brakes, and put air in the tires, but if your car gets better maintenance than you do, stop procrastinating, pick up the phone, and make those appointments you've been putting off. You are worth it!

Everyone knows that stopping car problems before they start is better and easier than repairing them. The same is true of physical problems. Whether you have a fear of what the doctor will find or you've simply put yourself at the bottom of your ever-growing to-do list, regular visits to the doctor will save you a lot of time on Google or WebMD. Whatever you're afraid of, whatever fear is making you procrastinate, you're stuck with it till you have more information. These are the kinds of worries that grow when you try to ignore them. Chances are that what you imagine is much worse than putting a name on what's wrong and dealing with it. And how stupid would you feel finding out that you have something that would have been easy to treat or cure—*if* you hadn't put off that doctor visit. Remember, I came within a gnat's butt of not getting my mammogram in 2012.

Feeling Fit, Fabulous, and Fantastic

When we greet one another and say, "How are y'all doing?" we're usually referring to physical health, which is essential to enjoying this next phase of life. Without it, the last bit of our cookie isn't going to be nearly as delicious—and it might not be as big, either. Let's take a look at some important physical factors that affect wellness, including a few that tend to fly under the health-care radar.

Heart Disease

The media has long focused on heart disease as a man's disease, but it's by far the leading cause of death among women, women our age especially. It kills one in every four of us and is especially prevalent in parts of the South and Southwest.[1] Chest pain, or angina, is the most common symptom, but it's not uncommon for women who have coronary artery disease to have no symptoms at all—until someone has to call the paramedics for you because you feel like there's an anvil on your chest, you've broken out in a cold sweat, and you're fighting to breathe.

If you have high blood pressure, high cholesterol, or excess weight—or all three—you have a much higher chance of having a heart attack. These risk factors tend to pile up on one another as we age. They also have more adverse consequences—with menopause, it's as if life catches up with us.

Fortunately, there are many things you can do to reduce your chances of getting heart disease, starting with making wiser choices about what you consume. If you still smoke, stop. Cook with less butter, more olive oil. Curb your alcohol intake. Opt for fruits and vegetables and fish and poultry over grits and gravy. Quantity matters, too—if you're in line at the breakfast buffet, remember that "all you can eat" is very different from all you *should* eat. For an upscale dinner restaurant, getting a reputation for being skimpy is bad for business, which is why most menus will serve up NFL-lineman-size portions that are much bigger than is healthy. When you eat out, you might choose an appetizer or a salad for your entrée, but I have another solution. I'm a member of the half-portion club. I eat half a meal and ask for a doggie bag for the rest—then I cross my fingers behind my back and tell the server it's for Chloe.

Know that even if you're careful, you might still have a problem. High cholesterol can be hereditary—it runs in my family. I've been prescribed cholesterol medicine, and I take a baby aspirin every night. For me, it's still an ongoing struggle, no matter how healthy I eat or how much I exercise.

Diabetes

If you've been doing battle with weight gain—and losing—you may be diabetic or prediabetic. According to the Centers for Disease Control, thirty million Americans have diabetes. Another eighty-four million—one in three adults—are prediabetic, meaning if the condition is not treated, they are on track to develop type 2 diabetes within five years. Here's the thing: diabetes is sneaky. Ninety percent of people who are prediabetic and a quarter of those with full-blown diabetes don't know it.[2]

Women over fifty make up a large percentage of those with diabetes, and it's killing us. It is the fourth leading cause of death for women ages fifty-five to sixty-four.[3] Type 2 diabetes is characterized by too much sugar in the blood. If having high blood sugar doesn't sound so bad to you, consider the sidekicks that come with it. Poorly controlled diabetes can have serious, even fatal, side effects, not just heart disease and stroke but also blindness, kidney failure, gum disease, and limb amputation.

Following a healthy lifestyle is the best way to stave off diabetes. My dad has type 2 diabetes, and I watch him exercise daily and carefully monitor his carb intake. If you are diabetic or prediabetic, your doctor may give you a list of recommended foods to enjoy and foods to avoid, but get to be a savvy label reader yourself when you go to the market. Added sugar doesn't always shout its name. Most of us know about sugar in desserts and soft drinks, but you'll also find it traveling incognito in many prepared and packaged foods, even savory ones like tomato sauce and salad dressing. Check nutrition labels for aliases, such as barley malt, sorghum, maltodextrin, agave nectar, blackstrap molasses, rice bran syrup, tapioca syrup, and high-fructose corn syrup. Increasing your physical activity level will also help fight diabetes. If you've been sedentary, start modestly and build from there.

All this being said, I'm not perfect. I don't claim to be. I love a Reese's peanut butter cup as much as the next girl, but I don't keep them in the house.

Osteoporosis

Osteoporosis makes bones thinner and weaker. As a breast cancer survivor, I am at higher risk for the disease. Actually, we're all at higher risk for osteoporosis just by being female and menopausal. If you're petite, that increases your odds even more. Although the disease can affect men, women are four times more likely to have it.

Studies have found a direct connection between declining estrogen levels and the onset of either osteoporosis or its precursor, osteopenia. If you smoke cigarettes, take prescribed blood thinners or corticosteroids, or have rheumatoid arthritis or hepatitis C, those factors increase your risk as well. According to the National Osteoporosis Foundation, eight million American women have osteoporosis, and half of us over age fifty will break a bone because of it.[4]

Like those dainty teacups in mama's china cupboard—the ones everyone's afraid to use because they break if you just look at 'em— osteoporotic bones are fragile. I have osteoporosis—a lovely parting gift from the breast cancer fairy. When I face-planted in the salon, I put my arms out in front of me to break my fall—that's a reflex—but my bones weren't strong enough to keep me from hitting the floor. They snapped at the wrist instead.

With osteoporosis, bones can break even without a fall, and it might not take much impact to make it happen. Just bending over could shatter one of the vertebrae in your spine. A cough or even a sneeze could crack a rib. I've seen that firsthand—I witnessed Eddie's mom breaking her ribs as a result of a coughing fit when she had bronchitis. It's something I'll never forget.

As the disease progresses, it eventually impairs your skeleton's ability to hold you up. Osteoporosis is a leading cause of pelvic fracture, which can mean the end of independent living. Frequently it means the end of life itself—one in three adults over fifty dies within a year of suffering a broken hip.[5]

That sounds like a scary future, but the ability to do something about it is in your hands today. Osteoporosis can be reversed—bones are living things, and like the cells in the rest of your body, bone cells are always renewing themselves. Upping the amount of calcium and vitamin D in your diet, as well as taking additional supplements, will help protect and improve bone health. I'm now seeing an osteoporosis specialist. I'm receiving bisphosphonate infusions yearly to build up my bone density, and I will be monitored regularly from here on to make sure they're working.

Exercise helps fight osteoporosis as well. It must be weight-bearing exercise—any workout that pits you against gravity is beneficial. This includes not only squats and dumbbell curls in the gym but also walking, tennis, yoga, and dancing. Have fun with it and try different things until you find something you enjoy. Just get out there and make it happen.

If you've recently suffered a fractured arm or wrist, or if your doctor suspects you are in a high-risk category for osteoporosis or osteopenia, a bone density scan may be in order. It usually takes less than half an hour, and it's painless. The test will detect weakened bones and susceptibility to fracture. When repeated over time, these scans will show a progression, and a picture will emerge. Your doctor will be able to tell how fast you are continuing to lose bone mass or how well diet, exercise, and supplements are working to build it back up.

Exercise

Let me start this section by saying I hate sweating almost as much as I hate exercise. And I'm going to be honest—there are plenty of days when I don't feel like it. I do it anyway. I don't want to hear y'all making excuses to get out of it based on how busy you are. With my hectic schedule of running a business, filming, spending time with family, and recuperating from my recent fall—if I can find the time to work out, so can you! Make yourself a priority—you deserve it.

Exercise combats so many health problems, and I always feel a sense of accomplishment afterward. The stronger your heart is, the stronger your muscles are, the better you'll be able to fight back against everything that will be coming at you—and you *know* challenges will be headed your way as you get older. Because being sedentary ages us, both mentally and physically, a regular exercise program can be the difference between one woman who's old at sixty and another woman who's still young and vibrant at seventy-five. And, let's face it girls, we all want to look and feel good for as long as we can.

Coming into this phase of life, everything just naturally starts to slow down. Incorporating moderate exercise into our daily routine benefits both mind and body. I'm not a fitness expert or a personal trainer, but I hope to motivate you to get started, or to keep going if you're already active.

Remember, however, that no matter what your personal fitness level may be, check in with your doctor before starting a new program or picking up the pace. Ease into a new exercise routine gradually. If your doctor recommends a half hour a day, it doesn't necessarily have to come all at once, especially when you're first starting out. Take a fifteen-minute walk around the block, then do it again a few hours later.

I haven't always made exercise a priority, especially when my kids were young. It's different now. As I've aged, and as I've seen life catch up with me, exercise has become more and more important to my daily routine and to my overall sense of well-being. It took me a while to figure out what I like to do and where I wanted to do it. I feel most comfortable working out at home, but that's a personal choice. What's important is not where you exercise but just doing it.

Some women love working out—I'm not one of them. What I love is the afterglow—that elated feeling I get when my workout is over. Even though I hate to sweat, I'm real proud of myself when I'm done. I'm always happy that I made the time. It gives me more energy and clears my cluttered mind.

Many women our age have body image issues. Getting your butt moving is important, but the gym can seem like a hostile environment. I'm as flustered as anyone else by the prospect of working out next to young strangers in a room full of mirrors. Being around twenty-three-year-olds in size-2 neon spandex as they flirt with grunting Hulk Hogan wannabes doing dead lifts is intimidating. Small wonder we stay home—we feel out of place and unwelcome, so we bury that health club membership card at the bottom of the purse.

Let it stay there, if you like. For your own fitness, think outside the gym—there are plenty of other daily exercise opportunities that don't make you feel like you're invading enemy territory. Here are a few:

- Outdoor Activity

   Getting outside for a walk, run, or hike is the cheapest and easiest form of exercise. If you're just starting out, stroll around the neighborhood and slowly build up your stamina. When you're ready, go longer distances or pick up the pace. If you're more advanced, try hiking with a friend or join an age-appropriate running group. The fresh air and heart-pumping cardio will do you a world of good. This is my personal favorite!

- Yoga and Meditation

   I love the mind-body connection that comes with yoga and meditation. If you're a beginner, take an introductory yoga class that focuses on teaching the basics. You'll get a workout while also improving your flexibility and strengthening your core. The meditation aspects of yoga have many additional wellness benefits. Quieting the mind and refocusing your energies is valuable.

- Swim Classes

   Swimming is especially beneficial for older adults and cancer survivors. The muscles we use in swimming can improve flexibility, while also toning and strengthening with each stroke. Swimming laps in the pool is great for maintaining heart health; even a couple of minutes in the pool has tremendous health benefits. The water is also easy on the joints, which is crucial for arthritis sufferers. If solitary laps aren't for you, sign up for a water aerobics class at your local community center or YMCA. You'll get in a great workout while making new friends. I love to swim!

- Work Out with a Four-Legged Partner

A dog is an exercise machine with hair. I adore Chloe, my puppy. She has brought our family so much love and companionship. She has also become an important part of my daily exercise routine. In the morning after my workout, I take Chloe for a really long walk. At night before I go to bed, I take her out for another extra long walk around the neighborhood. During our walks, we run into many friends and neighbors. Is this exercise, or is it a chance to socialize? I'm multitasking—it's both! Having a pet is a great way to be social, have fun, and stay healthy. Pets give balance and meaning to our lives.

Balance and Fall Prevention

I found out the hard way that we're at greater risk of falling as we age, and at greater risk of injury if we do fall. Our sense of equilibrium tends to decline over time, and health problems such as vertigo and ear infections can make it worse. A variety of prescription drugs, including some blood pressure meds and antidepressants, can adversely affect our balance as well.

Balance is a skill like any other—it gets better with practice, but you have to make the effort. Balance exercises can be an important factor in fall prevention. Disciplines such as tai chi and yoga improve it, but you can also do simple exercises at home. These include walking heel to toe, as if on a tightrope—or during a field sobriety test from the highway patrol. Another is to stand at your kitchen sink and pretend you're a flamingo. Lift one leg and place the arch of your foot on the inner part of your knee. Stabilize on your standing leg—without wobbling if possible. Odds are that you'll have a favorite side—this exercise is a lot more challenging if you stand on the nondominant leg instead. And before you get too full of yourself about how well you're doing, try it with your eyes closed. Just make sure the kitchen counter or some other sturdy object is nearby so you can catch yourself if necessary.

Reproductive Health

I'm always amazed when I come across women who haven't seen a gynecologist in ten years, maybe more. These are smart, educated women who are neglecting an important component of their health. The fact that your reproductive years are behind you doesn't mean that these organs are no longer part of your body. Ovarian cancer and uterine cancer are increasingly common after menopause. As with breast cancer, early detection is everything. Speaking of which, I shouldn't have to tell you to go get your mammogram, but I'm telling you anyway: go get your mammogram!

And then there's VA. You may be accustomed to thinking that the initials VA stand for either the Department of Veterans Affairs or for the Commonwealth of Virginia, but they also stand for something else. In the context of reproductive health, VA stands for vaginal atrophy.

Now, y'all, this is something my conservative southern mama would never discuss—and my grandmother would simply turn over in her grave. Any mention of delicate lady parts in her company was absolutely taboo. Our reticence is something we need to put behind us because this is a health issue that's a huge problem for us all. Not too many years ago, the same kind of stigma was attached to speaking out about breast cancer, and women suffered greatly because of it.

Vaginal atrophy, like so many health issues affecting women our age, deserves a lot more attention than it receives. It is nothing less than a silent epidemic. The Mayo Clinic estimates that at least half of all postmenopausal women suffer from it; other studies suggest that it affects 75 percent of us.[6] In other words, VA affects more women than the total number of veterans and three times the total population of Virginia. To put it another way, there are as many women with vaginal atrophy as there are people in the state of Texas.

Vaginal atrophy is characterized by thinning and inflammation of the vaginal wall. Thinner vaginal tissues are more fragile, making them more likely to crack or even tear. Milder symptoms include vaginal dryness, itching, and soreness or irritation. More serious VA symptoms include a burning sensation when you pee, leaking when you cough or hiccup, pain to the touch, and pain when you're with your partner. VA can leave you more vulnerable to waves of urinary tract infections, but its effects go beyond its physical symptoms. When intimacy hurts, this becomes a lot more than just a physical problem. It can impair your psychological well-being and can endanger even the healthiest and most stable loving relationship.

Only about a quarter of all women affected by VA seek medical help. Too many of us believe it's a sign of getting older and think it's a condition we're stuck with. We're not—there's a whole range of products that can alleviate the symptoms, and many of the most effective are available only by prescription. Nevertheless, it's not the easiest subject to talk about, even with your doctor. In a perfect world, your gynecologist will break the ice by initiating the conversation, but the world is a lot less than perfect. If you're having problems, speak up. If you can't bring yourself to mention it, include vaginal atrophy in a written list of topics to discuss when you arrive at your appointment, and ask the receptionist to slip the list into your file.

Mouth Health

During my battle with breast cancer, my oncologist prescribed a drug for me that removed all the estrogen from my body. It was essential to becoming cancer-free, but while I was taking it, my teeth turned gray and started cracking—just what you want for TV. Maybe it was just coincidence, but I've since spoken with other mastectomy patients who had the same experience. I spent a fortune getting my smile back—I'm sure it was enough for my dentist to retire to Tahiti and put all seven of his kids through law school.

Your eyes may be the window to your soul, but your mouth is a window into the rest of your body. An unhealthy mouth is often a sign of other health problems. Periodontal disease (inflamed gums) may be evidence of a whole host of serious health issues. The connection works both ways—gum disease is a reflection of some problems, but it also causes others. This is because bacteria in your mouth don't just stay there. They pack their bags and travel through the body each time you swallow. There are known links between gum disease and diabetes and between gum disease and coronary artery disease. Recent studies also suggest a correlation between gum disease and mental health issues such as stress, depression, anxiety, and Alzheimer's disease.[7]

These problems have a lot in common with osteoporosis. The same aging process that leads to bone loss in the spine and pelvis can produce bone loss in the jaw, creating periodontal disease and tooth loss. Because good oral hygiene is part of your body's best defense against a multitude of health problems, brush and floss regularly. An electric toothbrush and a water flosser are sound investments. Regular checkups with your dentist and your periodontist are even better.

Colorectal Cancer

Colorectal cancer is the disease no one wants to talk about, the one no one wants to get tested for, but putting it off can have tragic results. About 4 percent of us—one in twenty-four—develop colorectal cancer, and nine out of ten cases are diagnosed in people over fifty.

Because the key to beating this disease is early detection, women our age need to get a colonoscopy every decade—or more often than that, depending on your family medical history. When found early, colorectal cancer is treatable, even curable, and a colonoscopy can cut your risk in half.

Yes, I've seen the ads, and yes, you can send a stool sample off in a box, but colonoscopies are the most effective way to detect colorectal cancer at a very early stage. What the mail-in poop test cannot pick up is the presence of polyps—precancerous growths on the interior wall of your large intestine. Because your colon is empty, these growths are easily seen during the test and can usually be removed then and there.

And that brings us to the process of emptying the colon in advance of the test. There's no way around it: prepping for a colonoscopy is the pits. Subsisting on clear broth, tea, and pastel Jell-O (nothing red, blue, or purple) for a few days is bad enough, but inflicting galloping diarrhea on yourself for the last day or so is just vile. I try to remember that having to deal with cancer is a lot worse than that, and the peace of mind you get when you've checked that test off your to-do list is so worth it. So grab a good book or some gossip magazines, and be prepared to camp out in the bathroom, girls! Your reward: a flat tummy the day after.

Mental Health

You're going to feel better mentally once you take care of yourself physically, but you may still have problems, not that you'll necessarily want to acknowledge them. Talking openly about our own mental health is still unthinkable for many of us—for too many of us. Even when we know we have a problem, we don't say so out loud, for fear of being judged, for fear of becoming fodder for the gossip mill.

Those fears are not unfounded—it happens all the time. I've heard it whispered behind someone's back—we all have, as if it's a shameful secret: "She's seeing a therapist," or "She and her husband are in counseling." That perceived stigma keeps us from getting the help we need, but like any other kind of health issue, mental health problems don't get better when we sweep them under the rug and pretend we're fine.

From time to time, everyone struggles with something. That sorrow, that anger, or that heartache you're feeling could be about your marriage, or your kids, or your aging parents. It could be anxiety over your finances. It could be connected to a decline in your own physical health—and might be more directly connected than you know. Some of the meds that we take for physical ailments serve up depression as a side effect.

I'm usually sunny and upbeat—so cheerful that it can be annoying to others (or so I'm told). I was like Tigger in the Winnie the Pooh stories—positive, energetic, and bouncy—but my mental health took a nosedive while I was dealing with breast cancer. I was no fun to be around—I turned into Eeyore overnight. I didn't want to see anyone, so I hid out in my bed. At times I felt like I was at the bottom of a well, with no idea how or when I'd get out—or if I'd get out at all.

What helped me is what helps us all—talking about it. I talked to Monte. I talked to my family. I talked to my health-care providers. One reason why I immediately loved Jill Binkley, my physical therapist, is that she understood how cancer affects every part of your life, not just those bits and pieces of you with cancerous cells. The skilled, empathetic women on staff at TurningPoint, the breast cancer rehab center here in Atlanta, understood it too. As I struggled to feel like myself again and get back to something resembling normal, their words of comfort and reassurance made me feel better. Their willingness to take the download as I poured out my sadness and frustration—and yes, my anger—were exactly what I needed. They offered physical therapy and deep-tissue massage, but they were dispensing psychological therapy all the while.

If you need help, there's no shame in getting it. It's only fair to point out that when we confess our reluctance to talk about mental health, it's about the same as exposing our gray roots at the scalp—we're showing our age. Younger women are far less embarrassed to acknowledge the mental and emotional challenges they face, which is to say that they are quite open about it. My daughter, Mollie, sees a therapist regularly and feels better for it. Whether with a counselor, a psychiatrist, a clinical psychologist, or a friend offering an ear and a shoulder, talk out what's troubling you.

Spiritual Health

Maybe you would be more comfortable if that first mental health discussion was with your pastor. Most ministers get coursework in some form of psychological counseling during their time at divinity school. Moreover, they're trained to listen, both to what is spoken and to what's hanging in the air—whatever it is that you're trying so hard to avoid blurting out.

Those conversations can put you in closer touch with not just your mental health but your spiritual health as well. That may have been a part of your life that you let drop when you were younger. I sure did. When I was a much younger woman, it seemed to be the only piece safe to let go of when juggling for all I was worth, every single day.

I was trying to balance married life, children's lives, and a business, and I was wrung out. When Mollie and Cory were little, I was working Saturdays and Sundays at the shop, standing in high heels all day long, waiting on as many as eighty brides over the weekend. During those years, I was sporadic about going to church, and on those Sundays when I couldn't make myself get out of bed, I prayed that God was okay with sporadic because my legs ached, and I was exhausted.

One of the benefits of getting older is that I've been able to take better care of my spiritual health. Whatever your faith, whatever your denomination, it's important to have that quiet time with God. Every day. It can be reading the Bible in the morning or evening, but it can also be a devotional book, an app, or a prayer in your car at a red light. Some people think prayer has to be this huge event, and sometimes it is, but it can also be a continual train of thought. You can talk to God all day long, if that's easier for you. My conversations with God are more like an all-day conversation. I'm sure some days I give him a migraine!

I'm grateful for each day, and I say a prayer of thanks every morning. When I put my feet on the floor, I set my attitude. I make the conscious decision that it's going to be good day.

WHAT'S NEXT
Girlfriends' Guide

- **Look Out for Number One**

   Your body is a temple of the Holy Spirit (1 Corinthians 6:19). Taking care of that temple is your responsibility—don't expect your doctors to care more about your health than you do. That means stop putting off that checkup that's long overdue. Pick up the phone and get it on your schedule. The best time to do it was last month, but the second-best time is now.

- **Move Your Temple**

   Treatment for improved physical and mental health doesn't always come in pill form. Very often it looks a lot like exercise. Exercising is probably easier if you enjoy it, but the bottom line is that it's like brushing your teeth. It's hygiene. If you don't look forward to those sessions in the gym or on the treadmill, think like a Navy SEAL: you don't have to like it; you just have to do it.

- **What You Eat Matters**

   And so does how much you eat. Weight gain makes us look and feel older. Make the effort to consume more vegetables and fewer empty calories. Remember my half-portion rule!

- **Talk It Out**

   If you have physical or emotional symptoms that concern you, don't suffer in silence. Your friends, your family, and your physicians are on your side. Let them help.

- Nurture Your Faith

When you find yourself far from God, guess who moved? If you've drifted away from your religion, reconnect. Talking with God and taking time to center yourself spiritually will balance your life and remind you of what's really important.

5

God's Grace and Elmer's Glue

ℰddie Allen and I were college sweethearts. We met when I was a freshman at Columbia College in Columbia, South Carolina. Eddie was a cadet at Citadel, which is in Charleston, about two hours away. So was Randy, my brother—in a way, our marriage is all his fault.

Neither school was coed back then. Columbia College was for women only—still is—and at the time, Citadel was all male. There was a considerable amount of fraternization between the two schools. Randy called me one evening to say that he and two buddies were driving to Columbia that coming weekend, and could I please find dates for all three of them. After they piled out of the car, Randy paired off with my friend; Grant, who was Eddie's best buddy, was with my roommate; and I ended up with Eddie. When Randy asked me how it went, I told him that I thought Eddie was cute but pretty quiet. Randy reported back that Eddie thought I sure did talk too much. (Look where it's gotten me now, buddy!) It wasn't love at first sight or anything like that. Eddie and I saw other people from time to time, but we continued dating. Slowly but surely, our relationship grew, and within a couple of years we were engaged.

We were young, dumb, and crazy in love when we got married, and that was four decades ago. At our fortieth anniversary celebration, a family friend asked me how we'd managed to hold it together for that long. "God's grace and Elmer's glue" was my answer.

From the start, one thing we had in common was hardworking parents who'd overcome a lot of challenges. Neither of us was born with a silver spoon. My mom's side lost all of their family money in the Depression. And my dad's family never had it to begin with—his folks had seven kids to feed and barely scraped by. Eddie's dad was an orphan, and as a young girl, his mother had started working in a cotton mill to help make ends meet. All four of them held old-fashioned, traditional American values. To them, a promise was a commitment, and they honored it through good times and bad.

Their "I do" in front of the preacher was one of those commitments. Jean and Carroll, my mom and dad, have been married sixty years and counting. Lucille and Elvin, Eddie's mother and father, celebrated their golden anniversary before they passed away. Our parents gave Eddie and me the best, most valuable gift possible on our wedding day—a legacy of perseverance, of not giving up.

Eddie's mother was one of a kind. She was as country as corn bread, as they say, and many of my favorite southern sayings come directly from her. The woman would kill a snake and hang it on a fence post to bring on the rain during a drought. No kidding. Lucille often told me how proud she was of Eddie and me, and of our marriage—that we really seemed to like each other. She didn't have an easy life, and she and Eddie's father would go at it like cats and dogs. I'll never forget giggling one day when she looked at me through her lazy eye and said, referring to marriage, "Who the hell is happy?!"

Happily Ever After—or Maybe Not

Marriage is just plain tough, even when both parties are in it for the long haul. Sadly, not every couple—or each individual within a couple, for that matter—comes into marriage with that awareness, or with enough determination to see it through. In the salon, I help brides find dresses for their storybook weddings, and I've been doing it long enough that I can usually tell which stories will live on into happily ever after, and which ones will end in divorce court.

I see the eager young bride who is jumping into marriage, knowing that she's found her life partner. She's excited about her wedding, and she's peaceful in her heart as she chooses a dress to take this first step into their shared future. For her, the wedding ceremony is the gateway into marriage. She is taking her vows seriously and typically is honoring traditions from generations past. Often she intends to incorporate her grandmother's handkerchief, or her mother's veil, or some other heirloom into what she plans to wear.

That bride is getting married because she's in love, but there is also the bride who is in love with getting married. She's laser focused on the theatrics of the wedding itself and is devoting her full attention to the optics of the fairy tale. Because she believes that her wedding will surely be the single most important day of her life, she needs everything to be perfect. Every moment is to be micromanaged, but the most important thing by far is how she will look for her star turn coming down the aisle, when all eyes are on her.

This is the bridezilla who freaks out in alterations during her final fitting, when the wedding is just days away. As she obsesses over every stitch, it doesn't take much for me to see that her worries are not really about hemlines, beading, veils, and zippers. The curtain is about to go up on this glamorous event that she's orchestrated down to the last detail. But . . .

She has reservations, and they're serious. As her wedding day approaches, she's more and more worried about what happens when the show's over. She's worried about her own *What's Next*. The point of having a wedding is to get married, and she's belatedly realized that once she's no longer a bride, she's a wife—*his* wife. And as reality closes in, her misgivings come to the surface and her heavy, ambivalent heart is manifested in her behavior. This anxious bride-to-be is nursing a classic case of buyer's remorse about the groom, but the flowers have already been picked for her bouquet and the champagne is on ice, so she slips her cold feet into those Louboutin pavé silver pumps and walks down the aisle anyway.

This bride is destined to become one of my serial shoppers. I'm going to sell her three or four wedding gowns over the years. Much as I love repeat business, I'm sad for her, and for all the other brides like her. Regrettably, there are way too many of them. Some of them get it right eventually; some never do.

And some give up too soon. Millennials and Gen Zers thrive on change, and that's fine, up to a point. They expect to switch jobs every few years as a matter of course, and to them a whole bunch of life is as disposable as Ikea furniture, or at least always in flux. Unfortunately, that may include personal relationships. Many couples lack the tenacity to work out their differences, but marriage isn't always going to be a smooth ride. There will inevitably be bumps and potholes to navigate, and some of them will be big enough to rock your relationship to the very core.

A lot of what gets you through those jolts is sheer grit—your shared determination to stick it out. In other words, your pledge to honor your commitment to each other—for better or worse—just like you promised on your wedding day.

Figuring It Out

A marriage evolves—it has to because the people in it evolve too. Eddie and I are no longer the bride and groom we were on our wedding day. We're no longer the husband and wife we were thirty years ago either. Or twenty years ago. Or ten. And that is as it should be. I've changed. So has he. But we have embraced the changes in ourselves, and we've grown with them—together.

Of necessity, we've redefined our relationship many times over the years. The first time was when Mollie was a toddler. Working mothers were not yet the norm, especially in the South. As Eddie was growing up, his dad was the only breadwinner. His mom ran the household and didn't really work outside the home. It had been the same in my family when I was a kid. Now the two of us were trying to make parenthood and a two-career marriage work, but we were blazing a new trail through uncharted territory, with no family role models to follow.

Bridals by Lori was my dream. I'd gone all in on it with a big loan from my parents, but the business was hanging by a thread. New customers were rare, and those who walked in the door were at risk—I had to fight off the urge to dive to the floor and clutch their ankles to keep them from leaving. Eddie knew how important the shop was to me, and he was 100 percent supportive, which was essential. Although he was doing well at his job, I wasn't making any money.

Every penny I earned in the shop went to pay for someone to care for Mollie. At the time, there weren't a lot of childcare options where we lived, but I managed to find a woman who looked after kids in her own home. She was responsible and good with the children in her care, but that wasn't enough to keep me from crowning myself Guiltiest Mother in Atlanta. "Abandoning" a child to day care in order to work was eating at me something fierce. I drove away in tears every time I dropped Mollie off and headed for the store. "I'm such a terrible mom," I blubbered to myself as I boo-hooed in the car. "This child is my responsibility, and I'm stealing time away from her to run this struggling business."

I left her at day care in the mornings and picked her up in the afternoons after I closed the salon. We were open late only one evening a week—Thursday. On Thursdays Eddie had to pick her up—that was his only obligation.

One Thursday night I was with a bride, and I was thrilled to death because business had been even slower than usual. It was nearly eight o'clock, and I was in the middle of the appointment when the phone rang. It was the day care lady: "Well, are you coming to get Mollie?"

Eddie hadn't picked her up, which made me livid. I said good-bye to my customer as fast as I could, then jumped in my car. I cried the whole way over there. I cried on the lady's shoulder—she was very sweet about it, but I'm sure she thought I was crazy. Then I cried the whole way home.

As soon as I walked through the door, I demanded an explanation, and what Eddie had to say for himself made me even madder than I already was. If he'd forgotten his daughter, that would have been bad enough, but this was worse—he knew he was supposed to pick her up, he told me, but he'd been in a meeting.

It was a careerist, selfish thing to do, and I really let him have it. "Your meetings do not have priority over our daughter!" I shouted. And at that point I asked him to leave.

No, that's wrong. I *told* him to get out, using a lot of decibels and many four-letter words that I'm not proud of. I couldn't bear to look at him, and I didn't want him anywhere near me.

Eddie left in tears and spent the night in a hotel. Something I yelled must have gotten through to him because he met me early the next morning at the salon. And he came back a partner, eager to talk it out and fully involved from then on in parenting our children. He never did anything like that again. Bridals by Lori wouldn't be where it is today without Eddie, but most importantly, our family wouldn't be whole.

I know that I'm an exception. A lot of women in our tribe did not have as much support as I did from their spouses, either financially or emotionally, to follow their dreams. If you worked outside the home, statistics say your husband probably brought home more of the bacon than you did, even if you had a full-time job. But no matter what kind of day job you had, you were still pulling overtime because I'm willing to bet that you were the one who did the heavy lifting when the work-day was done. It's called emotional labor—most of it unacknowledged, and all of it unpaid—not just cooking and cleaning but also remind-ing him to call his mother on her birthday, sitting with your son to make sure he did his homework, consoling your daughter after her first breakup, and buying and wrapping the Christmas presents that were from him—perhaps even your own.

Not for Lunch

That phase of your life has come and gone. If he's no longer working, there's no reason why your relationship shouldn't be on a more equal footing—except that it hasn't been, and old habits die hard. Your husband may not have had his fair share of domestic responsibilities while he was working, but odds are he still shows no sign of shouldering more of the burden. Instead, he's in your space and in your face, all without lifting a finger.

It's easy to feel like there's a new intruder in what had been your domain, your sanctuary. You look at this man you're married to with so many questions: "Who *are* you, and why should I have to make you a turkey sandwich? How can it be that you're sixty-two years old and don't know how to feed yourself?"

This is the point at which many marriages founder—and then sink. I guess people do ask themselves, in Lucille's memorable words, "Who the hell is happy?!" Since the 1990s the divorce rate among people aged fifty and over has doubled.[1] This phenomenon even has its own name: *gray divorce*. Once the nest is empty, some couples conclude that, with their children gone, they no longer have anything in common. Having played the roles of father and mother for the past two decades or so, they've forgotten how to act like husband and wife.

If you want an equal partner but your husband still expects June Cleaver, domestic life can be a bit wobbly before the two of you find a new balance, but that's what needs to happen.

Otherwise, you're letting him have too much of that last bit of your cookie.

We've been talking a lot about self-worth, about valuing yourself, and about getting ready to dive into this next stage of your life with vigor and enthusiasm. I've already nagged you about investing in yourself and about "making the effort." A large part of that effort entails allocating more of your own time—and let's be clear, more of the family's financial resources—to caring for your own body and your self-esteem.

June Cleaver has left the building, girls, but from a husband's point of view, spending more time and money on yourself can look like trouble on the horizon. If you're focused on improving yourself and seizing the moment, he might interpret it as an unexpected and unwelcome outburst of selfishness on your part. He may even feel threatened by your intention to define your *What's Next*—unless you talk it out.

This is essential, y'all. You have to remember that your husband is looking at his own *What's Next*—the two of you have to talk out how his is going to fit in with yours. I probably don't have to tell you that answering that question may be difficult and even uncomfortable, but that's no reason to duck the conversation. There will be a relationship reset at this point in life no matter what, but the transition will be a lot smoother if you are straightforward with your partner about what your expectations are, and about what you need to thrive and grow together in this next chapter of your lives.

This is a time of new beginnings and a time to rediscover the connection you once had. You have to go on dates again and really start talking to each other. You have to fall in love again, or at least in like. And laugh—*a lot.*

Eddie and I just went through this. He sold his business and retired, which brought us to another recalibration of our relationship. I call it "For better or worse, but not for lunch."

Maybe you were sixteen when you thought you couldn't bear to spend even a minute away from your boyfriend at the time. You were head-over-heels crazy about each other. You did everything as a couple, holding hands, bodies pressed together hip bone to hip bone, as if you were Velcroed together at the side seams of your jeans. And you were sure it would be that way forever.

How'd that work out?

No marriage can survive the weight of that much togetherness. If you're everything to him and he's everything to you, that's a bough that's sure to break. Before you can live happily ever after with your partner, you have to be happy with yourself. That starts with seeing yourself as an individual, not as half of two. Nothing is going to work unless you like you. Remember that.

Eddie and I learned long ago to give each other space. Since his retirement, that has become more important than ever. Some days all we need is to go to opposite ends of the house. Sometimes just the sound of him chewing will send me running, and I know I'm not alone—I have yet to meet a woman our age who can stand to listen to her husband eating walnuts or granola at close range or, for that matter, anything else that's crunchy or lip-smacking, like ribs. Other times, even different rooms of the house are not enough, and one of us has to figure out how to be gone for a few hours. I can always take refuge at the salon, and going to work keeps me happy and focused. Eddie may even be there for part of the day. He oversees improvement projects at the salon, like the major renovation of our first-floor sales area. Even though we're working together toward the same goal, we're in different parts of the building. We have to be to keep the peace.

Beyond work, we understand the need to do things on our own. Both of us pursue outside interests that are ours alone, and we encourage each other to take the time to recharge ourselves separately. You should too.

Think of your personal assortment of likes and dislikes—what you adore and what you can't stand. It could be a hatred of football and a love of period movies, or vice versa. Think of it like a trick-or-treat sack on Halloween—it's never the case that you'll be able to share your entire bag with just one person. Your spouse will probably get the biggest part of that bundle—that's everything you have in common. But there will always be a bunch of stuff left over that's still in the bag—stuff that makes you *you*, stuff that makes you happy—stuff that he doesn't want any part of. And that's okay.

In the name of spousal togetherness, perhaps you've tried including your husband in some of these activities. If so, you found out pretty quick that he can be a real buzzkill if you drag him along like a hostage when he'd have preferred to stay home or if you make him watch another episode of *House Hunters International* with you. That's why friends were invented. Friends allow each of you to indulge your own interests. He gets tailgating with his buddies, seats in the end zone, and all the barbecue he can eat. You have girls' night out—group mani-pedis, a screening of *Downton Abbey*, and shopping for hours at the mall.

And you both get something to talk about later.

Getting to Know You (Again)

Talking . . . wives tend to want to talk out every problem, but men can just turn stuff off, and it drives me crazy—me and every other woman I know. Eddie is a lot more willing to talk now, but even that takes negotiation. I'm always ready to chat in the evening over dinner, after my day at the shop. Before, not so much. I'm just not a morning person. It's my only opportunity to think, drink coffee, and drag myself to exercise, but Eddie's an early bird. His favorite time for communicating is before breakfast, and sometimes when he wants to discuss a big idea, he hunts me down while I'm on the treadmill.

I really hate when he does that. He's barging in on my personal time. If you've ever tried starting a conversation with your husband during the fourth quarter of a football game or, worse yet, in overtime, it's like that in reverse. It can take a lot of willpower for me to get past being mad about the interruption, but I'll often take off the headphones and cut my workout short, even if I'm thinking, *Seriously, Eddie, you know I don't like talking at 7:00 a.m.!*

He almost always has something interesting to say, and that helps me remember why we got together so long ago. We're different people now, but after all the rough patches we survived along the way, we're closer than ever.

For us, the key was reconnecting with having fun in our marriage. I'm not talking about going out and riding Ferris wheels. I'm talking about the joy of everyday shared experiences, such as going to the beach or playing with our grandchildren.

In short, we rediscovered our laughter. You probably can tell that I love to laugh, and nobody can make me laugh like Eddie Allen. We laughed a lot before we got married, and then life intervened. There wasn't much to laugh about as we struggled to parent our kids through their turbulent teenage years. And then 9/11 happened. For weeks and months thereafter, you could have rolled a bowling ball through every retail store in the country—not just mine, all of them—and not hit a soul. The timing couldn't have been worse for us. We had just moved into our new building and had a child in college, and our finances were stretched to the breaking point. There wasn't any laughing then—we were scared to death of losing it all. It took everything we had to get through the day, but we stuck it out, worked it out, and talked it out.

Did we fight? You bet. Everybody in this world argues. Anyone who says they never argue with their spouse is lying. Either that or they've stopped talking to each other, which is worse. There have been harsh words and the slamming of doors in every marriage. Eddie and I were no different. We'd really go at it because he's as strong willed as I am, and that's saying a lot. But whenever we fought, it was always within the context of our determination to stay married, that legacy of perseverance we inherited from our parents. As angry as I might have been in the moment, I always had the comfort of knowing that when the smoke cleared and the shouting stopped, Eddie would still be by my side.

Ruth Bell Graham, wife of evangelist Billy Graham, may have said it best. Taking the major role in raising five children while her husband tended to the spiritual needs of the country, she was once asked—as First Lady Barbara Bush explained—whether she'd ever entertained the possibility of divorce. "Divorce? No. Murder? Yes," she replied.[2]

It's inevitable that, over the years, you've hurt each other. That kind of pain can be hard to shake, or as Dorothy Parker put it, "Women and elephants never forget."[3] But God asks us to do exactly that—to forgive and keep no record of wrongs (1 Corinthians 13:5). That's difficult, but it's necessary in marriage. You have to make the purposeful decision to forgive and move on or seek counseling to reach common ground.

Make the effort to turn the page and go forward together. This next phase of life has to start not just with laughter but also with forgiveness. Because so many things have changed over the years, and because recommitting makes a marriage feel fresh again, many women in this phase of life choose to renew their vows. Women feel like they've learned from experience and are ready to rededicate themselves to their partner with a renewed focus and with the savvy to do things right this time. Plus, it means I sell another fabulous dress. That's a win-win.

Faith can help a lot. Ecclesiastes 4:12 teaches us that a cord of three strands is not easily broken. This is a picture of united spouses with faith in God at the center of the marriage. Early on, Eddie and I were far from regular in our church attendance because by the time Sunday rolled around, both of us were often too weary to move.

Moving into this phase of life, that's no longer the case. We get up on Sunday mornings and go to church—together—and we have become more involved as volunteers in various church activities. Faith has strengthened our commitment to each other, and it has offered us a supportive community of people who reinforce it. If you're not currently involved in a faith community with your spouse, I recommend getting started. Surrounding yourself with a community and friendships that support your relationship is important, in both good times and bad.

To celebrate our fortieth anniversary, Eddie and I went on a cruise—we traveled on a riverboat all through Italy. As business owners, getting away is difficult for us, but we made it a priority. We were in Italy for twelve days, and our time together turned out to be a celebration of both our similarities and our differences. As I was soaking up all the art and architecture and history, Eddie got bored. I could have gone tromping through centuries-old churches and museums all day long, but he ODed on culture real quick. He was much more interested in the cafés and restaurants—the life of the places we visited. Eventually he found other men on the cruise to hang out with, so it worked out. We had an amazing adventure.

I am delighted to report that we didn't kill each other on the boat, and I'd been really worried about that before we left. I knew it was going to be close quarters in our cabin: it was only 210 square feet—with that little elbow room, the personal space we'd learned we each needed for ourselves was going to be hard to come by. Instead of getting on each other's nerves, though, we rediscovered each other as we explored new places together. We experienced a reawakening of our feelings for each other—a new appreciation for why we got married and why we still wanted to be husband and wife. We also reached an understanding that there's some fine print in our "I dos"—that "happily ever after" does not mean I'm obligated to listen to him eating potato chips or slurping minestrone or that he's duty bound to walk through HomeGoods with me.

As he turned off the light on the first night of our trip, Eddie turned to me and said, "I think we made it."

Wow! I drifted off to sleep thinking about that, and about how many powerful layers of meaning were embedded in that one simple statement. The most obvious was that we had finally made it to Italy—this trip had been near the top of our bucket list for years. But it went so much deeper than that. We made it—we built businesses. We made it—we raised a family. We made it—our children turned out to be good people who blessed us with grandchildren. We made it—we cared for our parents in the twilight of their years. We made it—we survived cancer.

And, of course, we made it to celebrate forty years of marriage. We made it—we made a life and a lifetime together, through God's grace and Elmer's glue. I fell asleep whole and grateful.

WHAT'S NEXT
Girlfriends' Guide

I realize that what I had to say in this chapter may not have seemed particularly relevant to some members of our tribe. You may already be divorced or widowed or separated, or perhaps you never married at all. Whether you're still married or not, there is one truth I hope everyone takes away from this chapter, and that is the first "rule" shown below.

- **Be Yourself**

    You alone have the recipe for this next part of your cookie. You're in charge, so own it. Add self-love and self-contentment to your own life first. Don't give that away, and don't bury your authentic, true self in the name of pleasing others, whether it's a husband of many years or someone you've just met. Be happy just being you and see what happens next.

- **Be Tolerant**

    Even if you have a healthy, loving relationship with your husband, you're not going to like him every minute of every day. And there will be times when he's not going to like you either. Give each other space to grow and explore as individuals, then come together and share.

- **Treasure Your Friends**

    Especially treasure women who aren't the spouses of your husband's friends. Friends are the bumper cushions of a relationship.

They give you a safe place to let off steam and a shelter when you need it.

- **Explore Your Passions**

  Whether it's working or volunteering, or a craft or hobby, don't abandon doing what makes you happy just because it's not your husband's thing. Do what brings you joy, and don't lose what makes you unique in your marriage.

- **Keep Talking**

  As you reset the balance between you and your spouse and reassert your place as an equal partner, keep your lines of communication open. Have fun sharing stories about your passions and adventures and be sure to laugh a lot.

- **Forgive One Another**

  You could not have gotten this far in marriage and in life without hurting each other more than once. Going into *What's Next*, you have to let those wounds heal. Make peace with your past—you can't start the next chapter of your life if you keep rereading the last one.

6

Wear Beige and Keep Your Mouth Shut

At a southern wedding, "Wear beige and keep your mouth shut" is the time-honored advice to the mother of the groom. To be frank, I'm 0 for 2 here. I look horrible in beige, and you already know that shutting up is not in my nature. Plus, Monte tells me that beige matches my hair color, and he doesn't say that as a compliment. He means that when I wear beige, I tend to disappear into a sea of blah—and I'm so *not* doing that.

We just talked in the last chapter about how a relationship between a husband and a wife goes through numerous resets as the years pass. At a minimum, there are adjustments when children come, as they become independent, and when they marry and start families of their own. As a mother-in-law, you will witness those changes not just in your own marriage but in your daughter's marriage and in your son's marriage as well. Those transformations are going to play out before your very eyes, and your children's recalibrations with their spouses will affect you as well. To be honest, I've had a lot of recalibrations lately.

That's not a bad thing—it's an opportunity. If your relationship with your children's partners started out poorly, it can get better. If it started out great, the dynamic between them as a couple is still going to evolve, and your place in the family dynamic is going to have to change with it.

I got off to a rocky start in my career as a mother-in-law. When Mollie was in her midtwenties, she and Jason had been dating for a while when he invited Eddie and me out to lunch. Toward the end of the meal, he asked our permission to marry her, and I nearly choked on the last of my grilled chicken salad. All the blood drained from his face. "*No!*" was not the answer he was expecting. The two letters just flew out of my mouth before Eddie could say anything.

I was being protective of my child and her future. This was my baby girl. Neither Jason nor Mollie had been out of college that long, and even though he was an engineer pursuing his master's degree from Georgia Tech, I worried that he was not yet ready to shoulder the financial responsibilities of marriage. "Are your student loans paid?" I asked. He shook his head. "Do you have other debt?" He nodded. (Jason never was especially chatty.)

"You're not putting those obligations on my daughter. Come back and see me when your ducks are in a row, and we'll talk again."

I'm sure Jason thought I was a something-that-rhymes-with-rich, and Mollie probably did, too, but he managed to get everything paid off within a year. They got engaged, and the two of them were able to begin their life together free and clear. Believe it or not, Mollie has thanked me many times for encouraging them to get their affairs in order before getting married.

That lunch might have been the last time I was able to talk that freely with Jason, to speak my mind directly and say exactly what I thought. He and Mollie have been married for almost twelve years. They are happy together (most days, ha!). He's very thoughtful and considerate toward her, and he's all about family—he's a true girl-dad, fully involved with his daughters. Looking back, he and I can laugh about that lunch, but he's still not a big talker. Of course, I talk enough for both of us.

Once your children get married, there's a new separation between you and your kids, and your relationship with them—and with their partners—is bound to change. Mollie doesn't tell me every detail of her home life. I no longer feel it would be okay for me to give Jason the third degree about his finances, nor would I expect that he'd feel obligated to give me an answer.

Child development experts have a name for this: *success*. Our job as parents is to raise our children to be independent so they can strike out confidently on their own. It's the opposite behavior that's problematic, a disorder commonly called "failure to launch."

Here's the thing, and it's a matter of simple physics: you can't launch without creating distance. Adult children have to put a healthy amount of space between themselves and their parents. That distancing, that parenting success, inevitably means a giant step away from the closeness you used to have with your children.

It's a step backward that you have to accept, but God knows I struggle with it, girls. Scripture tells us this about marriage: "A man will leave his father and mother and be united to his wife" (Mark 10:7). As part of the wedding vows, both partners promise to place their relationship with their spouse above all other relationships. During Mollie's wedding, when the pastor mentioned "forsaking all others," he wasn't just talking about ex-beaus and old girlfriends.

I was too busy dabbing my eyes with a tissue to fully get it, but he was also talking about Eddie. He was talking about Brenda and Paul, Jason's parents.

And he was talking about me. God meant for me to be one of the "others," to be among the forsook.

I don't do forsook well—more like the opposite. Since my children have gotten married, I've made mistakes, including some big ones that have been hard to put right. I don't have all the answers on how to be a good mother-in-law, but I'm learning, at least I hope so.

Boys and Girls Are Different— and So Are Their Moms

One of the things I'm learning is that there's a fundamental difference between having a son-in-law and having a daughter-in-law, and I have one of each. It's important to note that your son-in-law isn't your son, and your daughter-in-law isn't your daughter. They're family, but it's different. You didn't wipe their noses, bake birthday cupcakes, or cheer them on at sporting events; you didn't sacrifice for them to attend college. The relationship is different, and the boundaries are different.

During her rebellious teenage years, Mollie and I went through hell together. I didn't think either of us would survive, but we've grown extraordinarily close since then. Jason doesn't begrudge me my time with her. We still have outings, just the two of us, or with my granddaughters. I can show up at her house, and if there's a chair in the wrong place, I'll move it. If there's a crooked lampshade or picture frame, I can straighten it up and be absolutely certain that she won't be insulted.

When I'm invited into my son's home—and I would never go there without calling first or being specifically invited—it's different. Despite my son and his wife's best intentions, I oftentimes feel more like a guest. If my eye catches a lumpy pillow on the couch, I know I'm in trouble. Since I'm obsessive-compulsive about details like that, I fidget, and there gets to be a fresh set of teeth tracks on my tongue because I know I shouldn't mention it. To speak would be overstepping my position. I would risk offending Becca, my daughter-in-law, and that's the last thing I want to do.

Just the other day, I started talking about this with my mom, as if it was something new. While I was almost but not quite complaining, she just looked me and sighed. "Lori, I was in the same position with your brother and his wife," she said. "I didn't say what I thought for years. I hated it, but it was something I had to learn."

This kind of mother-in-law reticence starts even before the couple gets married. Once the engagement is announced, the bride and her mom become the CEOs of every aspect of wedding-event planning. The groom's family is pretty much off to the side. Sometimes they're entirely incidental, especially in the South.

I'm the exception, of course. I was blessed to be totally immersed in planning the weddings of both my children, but that's because of what I do. In my shop, I do see mothers of the groom who've been invited to help the bride pick out her gown, but they're very aware that their inclusion is optional. Many brides introduce their mother-in-law to me at the appointment as if they're doing her a favor by inviting her. On my sofa these women behave within the constraints imposed by their position far better than I ever could—in other words, they almost never say what they think. The watchword for the day is "Know your place—and stay in it." They're savvy enough to understand that it's all too easy for criticism of a dress to sound like criticism of the bride, so the most they'll venture is "Oh, you look gorgeous, honey." They're scared to death to say anything more—perfect training for their "Wear beige and keep your mouth shut" moment—the day of the wedding itself.

Nobody ever told me that "Wear beige and keep your mouth shut" doesn't end after the vows have been recited, but I wish they had. I'm naturally verbal and vocal—my head explodes when I have to keep my mouth shut, and walking on eggshells makes me crazy. I hate not saying what I think because that's how I am. That's *who* I am. I'm not assertive, I'm bossy, and have been since birth.

At Bridals by Lori, everybody is entitled to my opinion. Young women come in all the time with their hearts set on a particular dress, but they have no idea how many options are out there. Very often I can tell at a glance that what they think they want isn't going to be the best silhouette for their body type. I'll say, "That's one of our most popular styles this season, but I need you to try on this other gown. I think you'll see that it's more flattering than what you had in mind."

For forty years people have been coming to the salon for my point of view and my honesty, and they get it. And usually I'm right. I'm used to saying what I think, and I'm used to having people take my advice. Giving my honest opinion is how I make my living, and it's what I'm known for in the industry. Both fortunately and unfortunately, one of my granddaughters is exactly like me—and I expect her to be the president of the United States when she's a little older.

It's so hard for me to turn that off. As I leave the shop for the day, I often forget to flip the switch on my mute button and drape that hideous beige shawl over my shoulders. At family gatherings, if I do speak up and everyone's looking at me like I've dropped a Tootsie Roll in the punch bowl, I know I've put my foot in it—again.

Lord knows I'd be a hot mess as a diplomat, but being a mother-in-law calls for diplomatic skills, and mine can still use a lot of work. I *hate* not saying what I think, but I'm working on holding my tongue and praying about it. One thing that helps is to remember what this relationship looks like from the other side, and to think back to what it was like to be a daughter-in-law when Eddie and I were first married.

Steak Is What's for Dinner

Eddie was raised in the country. His family grew a huge vegetable garden, and they canned and preserved what they grew. Lucille, his mom, was as talented and creative as Martha Stewart, and then some. She fashioned handmade wreaths and knitted blankets. She made cakes and puddings from scratch, no recipe. The woman could whip up meringue for a hot banana pudding that had peaks on it to rival the Swiss Alps. No kidding. This is what I had to live up to, y'all!

She was a full-fledged domestic goddess—and then there was me, who couldn't even boil water. Lucille looked down on my lack of traditional homemaking skills—especially my cooking. Whenever Eddie's parents visited us in Atlanta, I was always delighted to let her take over my kitchen. She was a fabulous cook, but I never cared much about being good at it, and that bothered her a lot. I don't know whether she thought I was trying to poison her son or starve him to death, but she disapproved of how little I knew about cooking, and disapproved even more of how little I cared.

Every so often she couldn't resist making a snide comment about my cooking. Maybe she was frustrated watching me screw up all the time. On the other hand, maybe the idea that I was so la-di-da about something that mattered so much to her felt like a slap in the face—like a personal affront or rejection. Whichever it was, Lucille's potshots found their mark. More than once I retreated into the bedroom to cry about it.

One particular day in January, which is the busy season at Bridals by Lori, I stopped by the market to pick up steaks, salad, and baked potatoes for an easy dinner. Believe me, after standing on my feet for more than eight hours catering to a store full of brides, cooking was the last thing on my priority list. Lucille was visiting, and when I brought everything into the house, I could tell she wasn't thrilled by my dinner menu, since it wasn't made from scratch. I put the potatoes in the oven, threw some dressing on the salad, and put the steaks on the grill. Eddie, the kids, and I sat down to eat, and I had to call Lucille to the table three times before she sauntered over to take her seat. Much to my surprise, she cut the steak into tiny bites, and I watched in horror as she slowly chewed each bite with a look of disdain. As she brought her napkin to her lips after each bite, I realized she was spitting the chewed steak back into my good white linen napkins. Seeing the look on my face, Eddie devoured his steak as if we were at Ruth's Chris Steak House.

I can laugh about it now, but I still remember the huge fight that Eddie and I got into afterward. Well, maybe it was more of a harangue than an argument because I was chewing (no pun intended) Eddie out something fierce. I was going on and on about how mean she was and how mad I was until he looked at me real funny and said, "What do you want me to do? That's my mother."

Once he said that, it all clicked into focus. I realized right then that I just needed to shut up. When you're having a quarrel, you can't just rant—which is exactly what I'd been doing. You have to complain toward what you want to have happen, but I was carrying on about something Eddie couldn't do anything about. This was his mom—it's not like he was ever going to be able to change her.

I got a double dose of perspective that day. Not only was the steak tough, but so was my mother-in-law. The first thing that hit me was that I could handle it—I wasn't going to have to deal with Lucille but for a week or two at a time, and I could cope with that. The second thing that dawned on me was a question—was coping really all I wanted to do?

If my relationship with my mother-in-law stayed toxic, it was going to be contagious. This wouldn't remain a problem between Lucille and me—it would spill over into my relationship with Eddie. In fact, it already had.

It didn't take much to figure out that I shouldn't expect some kind of personality transplant from my mother-in-law. She was always going to be so country, and I would always be so . . . not. We had to arrive at a position of mutual respect and find our common ground—and over time, we did.

Having grandchildren helped a lot. It was extremely important to me that my children knew their grandparents. When Cory and Mollie were old enough, they spent a week or so every summer with Lucille and Elvin. They had the best time in the country, riding tractors and learning about growing tomatoes and watermelons. And of course, there were all those freshly baked fruit pies and mountains of meringue.

Time and maturity change everything. Eddie's only sister passed away at the age of forty-two, and toward the end of Lucille's life, she came to rely on me a lot. In fact, we talked on the phone every day—sometimes twice. By that time, I had become her surrogate daughter, and that was not a transition I could have imagined years earlier, as she was talking trash about my cooking when I was a newlywed. I grew to love her and her quirky country ways.

The Mother-in-Law

I'm now taking my experience with Lucille as a hopeful sign. We've all heard mother-in-law overreach stories—the woman who took it upon herself to rearrange the place cards at her daughter-in-law's Christmas table, or the mom who expected her future daughter-in-law to take a back seat—in her own car—so she could sit next to her son.

I was always determined not to be that woman. I didn't want to be the punch line, the butt of jokes. I wanted to be the cool mother-in-law, the one everybody got along with. That's not what happened. In the process of trying to win everyone over, I tried too hard. I overcompensated, overdelivered, overgifted, and overgave of myself. I became the smothering mother-in-law instead. If I walked into either of my kids' homes and they needed something, I made sure they got it as fast as Amazon Prime could deliver. Big mistake. I thought I was solving problems, but I was creating them instead. I had no idea that my generosity made everyone uncomfortable—both my children and the people they married. It was entirely my fault because I'm the one who overdid it. Because I'm generous by nature, it took a while to understand that my kids needed a healthy distance from me so they could make their own decisions.

I'm guessing that I've been the source of unhappy conversations between Mollie and Jason and between Becca and Cory, just as Lucille was the cause of arguments between Eddie and me. I never intended for that to happen, but just because a mom has good intentions doesn't mean she's not going to do something offensive.

I've been trying to work my way back, but it's going to take a bit. As the mother of adult children who have spouses and families of their own, I'm a work in progress. I want to be able to say to Becca and to Jason, "Look, I'm trying my best here, but this is hard for me. I have a very difficult time keeping my opinions to myself—always have. I recognize that sometimes I may say or do the wrong thing. Please understand that I don't mean to be hurtful. If I stumble, if something I've done or said has made you angry, that was not what I intended. If I've offended you, please let's talk about it together, just the two of us. What I want more than anything is to make the best of this relationship for each of us and for the person we both love."

This is one arena where I can take some pointers from my daughter. I'm very proud that Mollie has been able to develop her relationship with her mother-in-law, Jason's mom. She makes a point of inviting Brenda to do fun things together, just the two of them. Over the years their relationship has grown into a genuine friendship, and they now talk to each other freely.

The game changer? Mollie chose to truly embrace Jason's family as her family and reached out to Brenda—because that's what it takes for a relationship to blossom.

By opening their own line of direct communication, both of them have become more comfortable talking out potential problems one-on-one. I'm sure it makes life easier for Jason. Mollie has a better understanding of how her closeness with me can feel like exclusion from Brenda's point of view, and she makes the effort to avoid hurt feelings.

If the problem is big enough that you complain to your kids about their spouses, you have to expect that they're getting these gripes in stereo—both from you, and about you. For an adult child, being in the middle like that is awkward at best. At worst it can seem like a standoff between two biblical imperatives: forsaking all others versus honoring one's father and mother.

My ultimate desire is for both of my children to have solid, loving marriages that stand the test of time. I don't want to be the cause of dissension in their relationships.

The Stepmom

If you are your husband's second wife, you have an extra layer of eggshells to walk on. Your relationship with your stepchildren probably took some adjustment—maybe it's still tentative. When they marry, it's likely to get worse before it gets better. Don't expect your stepson's wife or your stepdaughter's husband to immediately be at ease around you. They may say things that are less than polite because they have no idea what to say at all, and they're petrified. This situation could stretch anybody's social skills to the max, and not everyone is going to be up to the task right away.

That said, this one's on you, Stepmom. Don't mistake self-consciousness or gaucheness or lack of tact as hostility. Give everyone time to be awkward, and make the effort to help them feel comfortable with you.

Not Always So Merry

Once your children marry, holidays can be miserable, and it's worth emphasizing that this is a particularly female kind of misery. Because women are the ones who set the family social calendar, it falls to us to come up with a plan. The uncomfortable tug-of-war begins as soon as the honeymoon is over: Who gets to spend which holiday with which set of parents?

In theory the simple arrangement of "We'll do Thanksgiving,

you do Christmas," trading off in alternate years, ought to work, but it's never that simple. There will inevitably be other factors involved. Siblings, their in-laws, stepmoms, and stepdads are often in the mix.

Bargaining toward a working compromise is a delicate negotiation, and everyone seems to prefer one holiday over the other. If your son's wife has a mom who clings to Hallmark expectations about Christmas, getting her to agree to do Thanksgiving instead, even if it's every other year, won't be easy. Some in-laws are just plain inflexible and are determined to celebrate on the exact date of the holiday, just as they've always done since their kids still believed in Santa.

I can be pretty inflexible myself—I don't want to compromise, and in some ways I don't feel that I can. With my parents now in their late eighties, every year is precious. Mollie and I still go to their house and decorate it for Christmas. I believe that the tree and gifts and pretty lights help them mentally, and I never know which holiday season will be their last. I also freely admit that I don't host Thanksgiving—I can't. It goes beyond the fact that I hate to cook and don't want little ones with gravy fingers anywhere near the fancy wallpaper in my dining room. There's a very practical reason: at Bridals by Lori, the Friday after Thanksgiving is one of our busiest days of the year. If it's 10:00 on Thursday night and I'm still cleaning up after serving roast turkey to a dozen or more people, there's no way I'll survive the Black Friday marathon at the store. I won't have the stamina.

For these and so many other reasons, the holidays, which should bring all of us great joy, bring exhaustion and unhappiness instead. The holidays generate animosity between mothers-in-law where perhaps there was none, and leave our daughters and daughters-in-law caught in the crossfire, having to choose. Across the country, thousands if not millions of young families stuff themselves with two turkey dinners every Thanksgiving, just to keep the peace.

Geography adds another layer of complexity. If you live closer to your children than the other set of in-laws, you probably see the kids and grandkids more often during the rest of the year than they do. To make up for it, odds are that they may feel entitled to claim more than their "fair share" of time together over the holidays. If the grandchildren are older, that might not be so bad, but what if it's baby's first Christmas?

This is one area where I am working on being flexible—even though I'm not happy about it. Both of my children live about two hours away from our home. I don't see either of my kids on Christmas morning. We celebrate with holiday brunch on December 24 instead. Cory's birthday is Christmas Eve, so that was always going to be a festive day, but it is still an adjustment for me.

Eddie and I have had to make our own traditions again, just the two of us. We attend church on Christmas Eve together and then host my parents and my brother's family for lunch on Christmas Day. I miss my kids and grandkids on the big day, but we make it work. You may have had your time-honored traditions with your children, but it's now time for them to create their own traditions for themselves and for their kids.

By now you've noticed that I haven't told you what to do here—which is so out of character for me. There are no easy answers to splitting time over the holidays. Families have to work out their own solutions, and I can guarantee that, whatever it is, the solution is unlikely to make everybody happy. I can also guarantee that the solution is going to change over time.

If you have expectations you can't get rid of about what the holidays are supposed to be like, just know that if you insist on "winning" the holidays, that victory may come at a price, and the people paying it may not be who you think. Even young children pick up on tension in a household, and do you really want your grandkids being stressed out by Christmas?

Nanny or Granny?

One of the most powerful forces in the universe is the love between grandmothers and grandchildren, and you may think there's no such thing as spending too much time with them. Actually, there is. I get that as working parents your children and their spouses can feel overwhelmed—that hasn't changed a bit since Eddie and I were raising Mollie and Cory. If you live near your kids and grandkids, it won't take a lot for them to wonder, *Rather than paying a teenager, since they're right here . . .* and then to ask, "Would you pick them up from school and watch them till we get home from work?"

Think carefully before saying yes to the request. You are the custodian of that last quarter of your cookie. Although I surely understand how rewarding it is to spend time with your grandchildren, it's supposed to be your turn now—finally. This *What's Next* stage of life should be about expanding your own horizons, and that starts with making plans and making the effort to get out of the house and get other events on your schedule. You still have so much to give to this world—your wisdom, your expertise, your experience. If you've now got time on your hands, it's yours—use it to make your life meaningful. To put it another way, I would hope that your grandkids are delighted whenever they see you, but that they don't *expect* to see you every day after school.

Of course, if your child is facing financial hardship or is a single parent, either temporarily or permanently, your being willing to step up and offer regular day care for your grandchildren can be a lifesaver. And if there's a family emergency or an opportunity for your child and their spouse to enjoy a night out or an anniversary getaway, there's nothing wrong with being ready to step in.

As a grandmother (Bella, in my case), I think of myself as the fun girl. My grandson is still an infant, but my granddaughters and I do things and have adventures together. I encourage you to help your grandchildren value the time they spend with you. That doesn't mean a steady diet of enrichment experiences—trips to Disney World and outings to the planetarium—but it has to mean more than flopping on the couch and watching cartoons together.

I made sure that both Cory and Mollie spent lots of time with my parents and with Eddie's parents, and it's important to carry that tradition forward. I want to give my grandkids not just my presence but a real connection with me—with who I am as a person. As they grow, I want them to look at me and at my life and be proud. I want them to know that I battled breast cancer and that I fell on my face— and that even though life events brought me down, I fought like crazy to get back up.

I'm still working on coming to grips with our changing family dynamic, with the understanding that Eddie and I aren't the center of the family anymore. Mollie and her husband, Jason, have become the center for their daughters, and Cory and his wife, Becca, will be the center for their infant son.

Just as I chose Eddie, I know that the Bible says that I'm to be forsaken, that Cory is supposed to choose Becca, and that Mollie is supposed to choose Jason. I also know that from a longevity stand-point, that's how it's going to turn out. Barring a tragedy, my son-in-law and my daughter-in-law will outlive me—time is on their side.

Even knowing that, it's sometimes hard to accept. I need to pray about it and release it to the universe. I need to pray that I can pull it back, that I can stop being obstinate-all-over-the-place-Lori, which I am much too often. I pray that I can give my children and their spouses space to grow. Mostly I pray that I'll keep my mouth shut, and that if I behave myself, God won't make me wear beige.

WHAT'S NEXT
Girlfriends' Guide

- **Find Your Filter**

    "Wear beige and keep your mouth shut" doesn't end at the wedding reception. When there is friction between married couples and their in-laws, the cause is often overstepping boundaries. Once your kids are married, you may still have a tendency to give advice—unsolicited advice. As hard as it may be, stop doing that. On the receiving end, unsolicited advice, a.k.a. constructive criticism, just sounds like criticism, period. There's no good way to do it, and it makes adult children furious because it makes them feel diminished—as if they are less than the fully responsible grownups they are. No matter how difficult it may be, you have to let your children live their own lives and make their own mistakes. That includes keeping your mouth shut if you disapprove of the choices they're making as a couple.

- **Step into a Different Pair of Shoes**

    If you're a mother-in-law, you've been a daughter-in-law. Try to imagine what it's like to have *you* as a mother-in-law. Think back to the relationship you wanted to have with your husband's mom—whether you had it or not—and try to work toward creating that with the people your children married.

- **Be the Change**

    Be the change you want to see in the relationship. There's only one person whose behavior you can alter, and that's yours.

Growing a better connection with your in-laws takes two, but it takes only one to start. Make the effort. You go first, even knowing you might not be successful.

- **Think Before You React**

    Even if your in-law tries to get a rise out of you with snarky comments, think before you fire off a retort in kind. These are likely to be words that you'll almost surely come to regret. You don't think of yourself as intimidating, but that won't keep your kid's spouse from feeling intimidated by you. That feeling is fear based, and those nasty wisecracks could be a self-defense mechanism, an indicator that somehow your son-in-law or daughter-in-law feels threatened by you. You can't control that, but you can control how you respond to it. Don't take the bait.

- **Establish Your Own Relationship with Your In-Laws**

    Whether you're a mother-in-law or a stepparent, leave room for the relationship to evolve on its own. Don't try to define your place unilaterally or stuff it into the role that you think you "deserve."

- **Talk It Out. Play It Out.**

    Avoid communicating solely through your son or daughter. Clear the air, if necessary, especially if you've overstepped. Find something fun that the two of you can do together, even if it's indulging your shared fondness for chocolate martinis.

- **As a Stepmom, Don't Try to Define Your Role Single-Handedly**

    Be open and approachable. Make it clear that you're not trying to fit into any cookie-cutter expectation of what your relationship ought to be. It may or may not have been Oscar Wilde who said,

"Be yourself. Everyone else is taken," but it's good advice just the same.

- **Work Out a Holiday Schedule in Advance**

    There's never going to be a perfect solution to this issue. Adjust your expectations. Be flexible and accommodating, if you can. You want to celebrate with your children and their other loved ones, not impose your personal footprint on the season of joy. I realize we have to throw the Hallmark vision out the window, but it's only fictional anyway, girls.

- **Speak Up When You Have To**

    As for wearing beige and keeping your mouth shut, all bets are off if you suspect abuse or infidelity in your child's marriage. All relationships go through ups and downs, and in general you should let the couple work things out between them but not when there is emotional or physical trauma. If you sense that your child is in crisis, don't remain silent. If necessary, offer to help your child connect with medical, emotional, or legal help. Mama, you'll know when to speak up.

Wednesdays with Mom

The seesaw always tilts. The teeter always totters. There inevitably comes a time in our lives when the balance tips and we transition from having our parents look after us to taking care of them instead. Because of tradition, and because we are nurturers, this task almost always falls to daughters, not to sons. Some of us have early memories of our mothers taking care of our grandmothers—both of them—not just their own mom, but their husband's mom as well.

For women our age, it's now our turn. If we are blessed to still have our mothers and fathers with us, there's no longer any doubt about which end of the seesaw we're on. We are the caregivers to our parents, to the older generation.

For years, my mom drove from Atlanta to Chattanooga every Wednesday to take her aging parents to lunch. She was working with me at Bridals by Lori at the time, and Wednesday was her day off. The drive was about four hours round trip, and that might strike you as a long way to go for lunch, but my mom never missed it. Her parents counted on her showing up so they could get out of the house and spend time with her. She set a beautiful example for me to follow.

The tilt happens for some of us later than for others. When I was diagnosed with breast cancer, my mom went with me to many of my medical appointments. As I faced surgery, I was grateful for her advice, and having her there with me was a great comfort. I was her adult daughter, and I was a brand-new grandmother myself, but I still felt that I was on the receiving end of the seesaw, soaking up all her love and wisdom.

That was several years ago, and the situation is very different today. Since that time my mother has had a stroke. She has better days and worse days, and better hours and worse hours, but she's limited in what she can do. She no longer drives and can be unsteady when she walks. She's also become a bit forgetful. She can talk to me in great detail about events that took place a decade or more ago, but she can't remember the key code for her own front door. We no longer leave her alone at home. Someone in the family is always with her because we're too afraid she might fall.

Even though my mom faces many challenges, I'm inspired daily by her grit and determination. During the day, she gets most of the help she needs from my dad, but unfortunately, he's had his own health issues, including heart problems. Dad has really stepped up to the plate to take care of Mom, and I've never once heard him complain about it, but I think he may be in a bit of denial about how much help she needs and how much more help she's going to need in the future. I also suspect that he could use a little help himself.

Not that he'd ever admit it out loud. Dad and I disagree on what name to put on this behavior: he calls it independence. I call it stubbornness. (Actually, I'd rather call it pigheadedness, and if I were talking about anybody else but my dad, I would.)

Most afternoons I go over to see my parents after I leave the shop. Bridals by Lori is open six days a week, and I work all six days. I have great managers and great people working for me, but I built Bridals by Lori from the ground up. For me, what happens in the store is personal. I still need to be there to oversee the business—and to film a hit TV show. I do the payroll and make decisions about what new inventory to order, and if the sink in the bathroom is dripping, I might fix that as well. I'm pulled in a zillion different directions all day long. There are always operational questions that only I can answer, and I need to be available to assist consultants and talk with brides and their families in between takes of filming the show. In a way, I'm like Mickey Mouse. If you visit Disneyland or Disney World, you expect to see Mickey. When people shop for a gown at Bridals by Lori, they expect Lori to be there.

The one day I'm off is the day the shop is closed: Wednesday. That's my sacred day with Mom. Before her stroke, doing stuff together on the occasional Wednesday was already a tradition between us, but we didn't go out every single week. Since then, I wouldn't think of missing our "date." I want to give Dad a bit of a break, but more than anything, I want to get her out and get her active because, otherwise, she's pretty much confined to the first floor of her home. Steps are a struggle for her, and their driveway is so steep that it's impossible for her to navigate it without falling. She can't go upstairs and she can't go outdoors—it's almost like being under house arrest.

And then there's the elephant in the room: I can't imagine skipping a Wednesday with Mom because I don't know how many more Wednesdays I have left with her.

The Mirror Test

When you have aging parents, the Mirror Test will always be in the back of your mind. Once their days on earth are over, you have to be able to look at yourself in the mirror and be at peace. You have to be sure that you did everything you could to take care of them, and that you did it in the absolute best, most loving way you knew how. No regrets. No if-onlies.

For me, that now means skipping a Wednesday with my mom is out of the question. Even if I'm dog-tired and I'm leaving a bunch of business stuff undone, I live in fear that the one Wednesday I don't go—the one Wednesday I make other plans—will turn out to have been the final one. And the weight of that would be more than I could bear. If only I'd gotten off the couch . . . the guilt from missing that one last chance to be with Mom would be on my conscience forever—for me, that's the biggest if-only of them all.

Beyond the imperative of the Mirror Test, "Wednesdays with Mom" also has a positive side: the simple joy of it all. Mom enjoys these outings to no end, and it makes me happy to make her happy. I feel responsible for making her day wonderful, and I go out of my way to do just that.

I want both of my parents to enjoy life as much as they still can. I consciously take up that burden—personally—every morning when I wake up. Mollie and Cory keep telling me not to think that way, that I'm putting too much stress on myself, but the pressure I feel isn't voluntary—it comes with the territory, and it just shows up. On an intellectual level, I know that I can't take this responsibility entirely on my own shoulders. In the same way, I kinda get it that I can't "make" my mother happy, in the sense of forcing or compelling her to have a good time. But that's Lori's head talking, and la-la-la-la-la, Lori's heart is not listening.

When I think back to all the things Mom did to make me happy as I was growing up, like our Friday afternoon snack and shopping dates after school when I was a little girl, making her happy now is exactly what I'm going to do. That's what being a daughter on the giving end of the seesaw is all about.

Every Wednesday morning at 10:30, I pull up in front of their house. Mom is dressed and ready to go. We always head for the same destination: the mall. Why the mall? It's climate-controlled, and it's flat. With weakness on her right side from the stroke, she should have a walker, but she won't get one, so I hold her arm and she holds my hand, and we walk. We look in the windows, and if she says, "Lori, that's pretty," we'll stop. My mom is a great shopper—she will shop me from one end of that mall to the other. The woman could out-shop a teenager with her daddy's credit card. She also has a specific itinerary. Each week we have to make the rounds to visit her people—the salesladies in the petite departments. She always finds something to buy. Usually it's a pair of black pants. I'm sure she has more black pants than she'll ever need, but I don't care. She could buy five hundred pairs of them—if it makes her happy, it's fine by me. After we've shopped and said hello to all the ladies in the petite departments—*all* of the petite departments, I take her out for a nice lunch and then take her back home to visit awhile.

Our parents' golden years present challenges that we all have to face and think through. For me, this is a joyful responsibility. But if your relationship with your mom and dad has not been as positive as mine, that doesn't absolve you of your obligation. Remember, Exodus 20:12 tells us to honor our parents, and it's not a suggestion. It's a must, period.

Doing What's Best Isn't Always Easy

I have no idea how much longer my mom will be able to enjoy our outings together. As she and Dad inch their way toward their ninetieth birthdays, the challenges they face will become bigger, not smaller. I would like very much to bring in outside help, but that has become a very sore subject.

Which is to say my father won't hear of it.

He's fiercely independent, and I love that about him—it's so much a part of what makes him who he is—but it drives me crazy that he refuses help of any kind. Right after Mom had her stroke, my brother, Randy, and I hired somebody to come in and cook for them. Dad fired her within days, and she turned out to be just the first in a series. I kept trying, but Dad got rid of every one of them. I even found a woman to come in most afternoons, take Mom shopping, and help with meal prep and some of the chores. I figured she'd be perfect, but when I tried to talk to him about it, Dad put on his sternest face and shook his head. "I don't want that woman in my house," he declared firmly.

Mollie and Cory do what they can, but both of them live hours away and have young children to care for. Some Wednesdays during summer vacation, when school's out, Mollie and her daughters come mall-walking with us, but she is also running her own business, so it's a real time sacrifice for her. Eddie will help when I ask him, and I probably should ask him more often. Randy pitches in when he can, which is always an enormous help, but he travels a lot for his job. Sometimes now, on Sundays, he'll cook and have our parents up to his home. Dad loves it because it gets him out of the house. With Mom venturing out so seldom, he's a bit housebound himself.

The house. Their house is a problem. They've lived in it for about a dozen years. They're comfortable in it, and they like their neighbor-hood, but their driveway is like the Matterhorn. Even getting the garbage down to the street is a challenge. Mom has told me more than once that she'd be fine with moving into a patio home in a senior living community, but Dad refuses. She looks at it as a new social opportunity—a chance for her to have lots of other people around to talk to. Dad takes the opposite view. He thinks of it as giving up, as the beginning of the end. Out of the question. "Just stick me in a hole," he says, "because I'm not going."

I know where that comes from, I think. My father has always been the patriarch, our family CEO, and he's old-school about the expec-tations he associates with that title. As the leader, he believes that he must not allow himself to appear fragile or vulnerable or less than completely on his game. A move into a retirement community is like allowing someone to come in to cook or clean, only worse. It's admit-ting a need or a weakness, and that's something the commander in chief would never do.

I also worry about my dad driving in Atlanta traffic. Heck, I worry about anyone driving in Atlanta traffic. At eighty-seven years old, his reflexes are not what they once were.

It's all stressful. I have nights when I sit bolt upright in bed, wor-ried sick about both of my parents. My head's in overdrive, swamped by nightmare images of the myriad things that could go wrong—in the house, out of the house, in the bathroom, in the kitchen, in the car. I worry even more about the gulf between what I think I should be doing to help them and what my parents, Dad especially, will allow me to do. I don't want those undone things to become my if-onlies.

I'm very aware that I'm not the only one trying to navigate this issue. Many people in my circle of friends are coping with similar sit-uations. Everyone has cobbled together various ways of dealing with it, but no solution lasts for long, and nobody is entirely happy with how it's going. Monte's mom recently passed away after a long battle with Alzheimer's, so he then went ahead and brought in full-time, live-in help for his father. That's not a choice that's open to me—not with Dad the CEO. The last thing I want to do is to take over his life, or my mother's life. It would offend them greatly, and their dignity is as important to me as their safety. Nevertheless, the sense of power-lessness I feel can be overwhelming, and I know that many women our age feel the same way. I'm contending with these feelings the only way I know how—one day at a time, always mindful of trying to make the right choices, not just in the moment but in the long run.

Navigating Different Needs

Doing what's right is hard enough if only one of your parents is still with you, but it can be much more difficult with two. My parents are still together, and that is indeed a blessing, but each of them faces distinct health issues that have different implications for their future, both in the short term and the long term. Mom's problems affect her ability to function on a daily basis. Dad is a few years older, and his problems may be potentially more serious. If Mom were no longer able to live at home, he'd be lonely, and he would need someone to see to his meals, but I wouldn't be concerned about his physical safety on an hourly basis. On the other hand, if he were to have a serious health event and had to be hospitalized or placed in a rehab facility for even a few days or weeks, my mom wouldn't be able to get along on her own.

If either of my parents needed immediate medical attention, Dad would be able to dial 911, but it's not at all clear that Mom would know how to reach the paramedics. I'm about to get each of them an emergency pager. And yes, I know that there is zero probability that my father will actually wear his, but if something were to happen to him, Mom could probably manage to summon help by pressing the button on hers. Those "I've fallen, and I can't get up!" TV ads are beyond corny, but, for me, every added bit of peace of mind helps.

I know that peace of mind may be elusive from here on. My family will have to keep thinking through what each of my parents needs, independently as well as together. Inevitably, this will involve frequent reevaluation as circumstances change. And that's the key for all of us who are helping older parents—being as responsive as possible, anticipating whenever we can, but knowing at the same time that unexpected problems are likely to pop up.

The Book, the Directives, and the Conversation

Having been a CPA and a real-life CEO for a major corporation, my dad is used to being organized and in charge. Our entire family leans on him for business advice and wisdom. In fact, he still does people's taxes. He keeps a book that supposedly has everything we would need to know in case he were to become incapacitated—how to access bank and health records, Social Security, and other important documents. It's current, as far as I know, but I've never seen it.

Lots of parents don't have a book, or anything like it. What I'm learning from conversations with friends who have recently lost one or both parents is that many people of that generation, once they hit their eighties, seem to go out of their way to avoid the topic of end-of-life planning entirely. This is potentially a huge problem for us, their children, because we're going to have to deal with it eventually if they have not.

I'm going to suggest here that you do something that I haven't been able to do yet, and that is to initiate a conversation with your mom and dad about their health, about what to do if it starts to seriously decline, and about what happens after that. It's a difficult conversation to have, but it has to happen. The timetable for every family is different, but it's something I know I can't put off much longer.

How do you bring up the subject? Each of us has to find our own way. My plan is to couch it in terms of Eddie and me and our children—their grandchildren—as a way to get the conversation started. "You know, Dad, especially after my fall in the shop, Cory and Mollie have been encouraging Eddie and me to better communicate our plans. They want to know what our wishes are for hospitalization and eventually for end-of-life care. We're putting together a book like the one you have, and they've suggested some questions they want us to answer. This is the kind of information that's in your book, right?"

Am I sure it will work? Nope, but my hope is that it's at least a way to get them to talk about it. It does concern me that I have no idea what's in my father's book. I would feel much better if I were aware of its contents before I ever had the need to open it.

In addition to financial and insurance information, I'm hoping that it contains advance directives and a POLST for each of them. An advance directive, sometimes called a living will or power of medical attorney, is a legal document. It officially designates a friend, family member, or other surrogate to make health-care decisions on your behalf if you cannot speak for yourself. Having been through a mastectomy and its aftermath, as well as the face-plant that left me unconscious for several minutes and could have been much worse, I feel strongly that having an advance directive is essential—not just for your parents but for yourself as well.

A POLST is a medical document, not a legal one, and works in tandem with an advance directive. POLST stands for Physician's Orders for Life-Sustaining Treatment. In some states it may be known by a different acronym—MOLST (Medical Orders for Life-Sustaining Treatment), SAPO (State Authorized Portable Orders), or TPOPP (Transportable Physician Orders for Patient Preferences) are a few alternates. They all have the same goal: for people at risk of having a serious medical emergency within the next few years, a completed POLST form will clearly tell any health-care professional who may treat them what medical procedures they want and don't want.

The forms vary from state to state, but most ask about procedures such as tube-feeding and artificial respiration and about palliative or comfort measures when recovery is no longer medically possible. They may also cover blood transfusions, dialysis, and other treatments. People who make these choices for themselves, while they are well enough to do so, give their family members great peace of mind. Loved ones are relieved of the burden of making snap decisions in a critical situation, when time is of the essence and they are under great emotional stress.

The POLST form is usually filled out with a primary care physician, but it may be completed with a member of the clergy as well. These skilled professionals are experienced at guiding seniors into having "the conversation" in a way that family members often cannot.

This is a highly personal choice. Some people may want to take advantage of every medical breakthrough to give themselves the best chance at survival; others are focused on quality of life and can't bear the idea of being hooked up to feeding tubes or breathing machines. Life is precious, and medical science can and does work miracles, but having a say about how many of those miracles would be deployed on your behalf should be up to you.

Last Wishes

Dad's generation tends to be real tight-lipped about weighty conversations. This includes end-of-life issues and last wishes. I have several friends who have suddenly lost a parent. When they went through their parents' papers, they were shocked to find that there was absolutely no indication of funeral or burial arrangements. It's bad enough to be planning a memorial service for a parent on short notice, while you're grieving, but it's so much worse if you have no idea whether the choices you're making are what they would have wanted.

With my dad, I was very doubtful that I'd ever be able to get him to talk about what he would want in the way of a funeral. If he were to voice those thoughts aloud, it would make the possibility too painfully real in his eyes. And, for me, it's just more emotional than I can bear.

Mollie was the one who was brave enough to broach the subject. She's pretty fearless that way—she makes me have hard conversations on tough subjects, even when I don't want to, and she did the same with her grandfather. The last time my dad was hospitalized, she pretty much pinned him down, right there in the cardiac ward. He was trapped, and although he was reluctant to talk about it, it was obvious that he'd already given it some thought. The conversation was emotional, and they both cried, but I now know who he wants to officiate at his services and what music he wants us to play. Now we need to have the same conversation with my mother.

The Final Transition

In the end, there is just faith and family. We may wish to say our last words to our mom or dad while they're still fully conscious, but medical reasons may make that impossible. Even with a loved one who is alert, our awareness that our time with them is ending may leave us too emotional to speak. When Eddie's mother was in the hospital for the last time, he went to visit her there. She looked at him and asked, "A penny for your thoughts?" He couldn't say anything—he was too choked up—and she passed before he had one last conversation with her. More than a decade later, he still says that it was one of the biggest mistakes of his life. I keep telling him that he shouldn't beat himself up that way, that his mother surely knew how much he loved her, but it still eats at him—it's his if-only.

If your relationship with your dying parent has been difficult, there will never be a better time—or another time—for forgiveness. All of your bottled-up anger has been eating away at you from the inside for far too long. It's toxic, and it has probably poisoned your relationship not just with your mother or father but with others as well. No matter what your parent did, beneath all their bad behavior was someone who was overwhelmed—by circumstances, by finances, by deceit, or by disease—and who made bad choices as a result. On some level they were trying to do their best—even if their best was not very good, even if it was misguided, even if it had hurtful consequences for you and for others.

This is the time to open your heart to your estranged parent, to one of the people who brought you into being. Put down those heavy bags of hate and anger and forgive—whether or not an "I'm sorry" will ever be coming back your way. If you can't bring yourself to do it for them, do it for yourself. Spare yourself the if-only that will surely be with you forever—until you yourself are on your own deathbed. Forgiveness is as much a gift to you, the surviving child, as it is to the parent who is in the last days or hours of life.

During the transition from life to death, there is often a stage when the heart still beats but the eyes are closed and there is no visible reaction to words or touch. If someone takes a turn for the worse and appears unresponsive, it may be a comfort to know that medical science now believes that hearing is the last sense to go. Put your mouth close to your parent's ear and say what you need to say. Pray with them and read their favorite verses. Your mom or dad will recognize your voice even if they can no longer acknowledge it.

When death is near, some people want you to hold their hand. Others wait, seemingly on purpose, till you've left the room for a small break, so they can slip away alone. When that beloved heart stops beating, know that the sadness is with those of us who are left behind, not with the souls who have departed. We will mourn because we miss them, but what we are mourning is the emptiness left in our own lives. When a parent has accepted Christ, we need to celebrate the life that has transitioned, and most of all, we need to celebrate their eternal life with God in heaven.

WHAT'S NEXT
Girlfriends' Guide

- **Give Your Parents Good Times on Their Own Terms**

  I've been doing Wednesdays with Mom for a while now, but here's something I learned from Monte. As he was caring for his own mom, he gave me one of the best pieces of advice. It's also one of the hardest to follow. If you plan an outing with a loved one, let them have the day they want, not the day you want them to have—even if it means repeating the same outing time after time. When parents find that coping with change is becoming difficult and even scary, there is great comfort in things that are familiar. If your loved one is no longer fully able to live in your world, the only way you'll connect with them is by jumping into theirs and being in their reality with them for a time.

- **Take Care of Yourself as the Caregiver**

  Don't be collateral damage. It's a wonder of modern life that we often let ourselves believe that we're the only ones going through this stage. We're not, of course, which means that this is the time to reach out to friends for emotional support. Find someone who gets it—it could be a friend who is also caring for aging parents or someone who's done so recently. They may or may not have practical suggestions, but they will surely have a sympathetic ear and be ready to sit down with you over lunch and listen and hand you a tissue when you need one. For me, having Monte's understanding, support, and listening ear during this difficult season of life has been so important. And I've tried to provide the same support for him.

- ## Care at Home: Share the Load, Share the Love

Eldercare is taxing, both physically and emotionally. This is especially true if a parent has mental health issues in addition to physical limitations. Don't try to shoulder all the care by yourself.

Many of us have siblings who don't live nearby, but there will surely be times during the year—a vacation or summer break—when they're able to pitch in in person. They may also be able to help in other ways, such as paying for respite care, adult day care, or in-house help. If you keep a checklist of tasks that need to be accomplished—cooking, cleaning, bathing and personal care, trips to the doctor, exercise, staying with a parent overnight—figure out which are best for you to delegate. Let others know what they can do, what you expect them to do. Nobody gets a pass because of geography.

Enlist the help not just of siblings but of spouses and older grandchildren as well. There will always be tasks that others can do. Document what you do and the schedule on which you do it. A lot of this help may involve personal hygiene. You can't be above doing what needs to be done to care for those you love. For both my mother and mother-in-law, I've had to put on a bathing suit to give them showers when they weren't able to do it alone. Be sure to list the tasks that sometimes fall through the cracks and the jobs that are physically beyond your capabilities. Although I could help bathe my mom and mother-in-law, many women wouldn't be able to assist a larger man into or out of the tub without risking injury to themselves. When someone asks how they can help, don't be shy—tell them. Let them know how frequently their assistance is needed—daily, weekly, monthly. It's a guy thing, I think, but men often don't volunteer—they wait to be asked. So ask, and be as specific as you can about how much help you need and how often.

- Get Outside Help If Possible

  Caregiving help varies markedly from one community to another, in quantity, quality, and cost, but state and local agencies can connect you with what's available. Insurance may cover some services, in whole or in part. Look into respite care, adult day care, help with cooking and housekeeping, and, if necessary, hospice care.

- Promote Dignity and Safety

  Many parents want to "age in place," remaining in their homes for as long as possible. Make it safer for them to do that. Up the wattage of the lighting in the kitchen. Have raised seats installed on the toilets and safety grab rails installed in the tub and shower. If you see signs of Alzheimer's or dementia, you may also want to remove the locks from the bathroom doors and put a safety catch on the drawers where the knives and the car keys are kept. Monitor prescriptions—at some point it may become unwise for your parents to self-medicate. Watch for indicators that their disease is progressing. If your loved ones start leaving the stove on, it may be time to remove the knobs or consider relocation.

- Help Your Parents Relocate to Preserve Their Independence

  If your parents have a too-big house with too many steps or if they're too far away, either from you or a sibling, or even from the grocery store, it's best if they make the transition to a smaller, more convenient living arrangement while they're relatively healthy. Sooner is better than later. A patio home or single-story townhouse with walk-in or roll-in showers and other barrier-free amenities will allow them to preserve their independence for as long as possible.

- Make a Plan, Make Several

You need to know what to do if your parents can no longer speak for themselves. If they have not already done this on their own, make plans for declining health, living arrangements, long-term health care, and last wishes. If possible, try to be specific—which rehab facility, which memory-care facility, which visiting-nurse service, which memorial park.

The best time to make those plans is well before they're needed. Encourage your parents to participate in making these arrangements to the best they are able. To be sure, these are hard conversations to have, but they're even harder when you must have them under duress.

At the outset don't worry that the plan isn't "perfect" or perfectly complete. Even if it's not exactly what you want or what they want, you at least have a point of beginning. Keep adding more information as you go. Plan for a number of alternative possibilities, especially if both parents are alive. One parent may have a very different health-care prognosis than the other. They may also surprise you by having very different last wishes.

Know how to find the plan when you need it, but don't let it languish in a drawer. As parents age, their living requirements and health-care needs may change quickly. If there has been a change in status, make sure the plan is still applicable. Also make sure it's dated, so if there are multiple versions, you know which one is current.

Don't Make a Promise You Can't Keep

If they sense their health is declining, your dad or mom may ask you to promise that you'll never place them in an assisted-living facility. Avoid doing that. My grandparents asked this of my mom, and they both ended up needing the care only a nursing home could provide. To this day, my mom still feels guilty about it even though she did what was best and necessary for their health.

The need for assisted living is often more about mental health than about physical disability. "Longer lifespans are perhaps one of the greatest success stories of our modern public health system," says Nora Super, senior director of the Milken Institute Center for the Future of Aging. "But along with this success comes one of our greatest challenges. Our risk of developing dementia doubles every five years after we turn 65; by age 85, nearly one in three of us will have the disease."[1] The 2019 Milken Institute Report, "Reducing the Cost and Risk of Dementia: Recommendations to Improve Brain Health and Decrease Disparities," estimates that the economic cost of dementia will exceed $2 trillion—and that women will bear more than four-fifths of that cost.[2] In its early stages, home care for a loved one with dementia is manageable, but it becomes increasingly difficult as the disease progresses.

Within the home environment, there are limits to what even the most dedicated caregiver can do. She can easily get swamped by the need to deal with the incontinence, wandering, and/or sudden outbursts of rage and physical violence that are often characteristic of advanced stages of the disease. It can be so overwhelming that delivering around-the-clock care becomes more than one person can handle—so much more that the health of the caregiver is sacrificed in the attempt to provide it.

Eventually many dementia patients will need more assistance

and support than can be provided at home. At the same time, they may begin losing the ability to recognize their surroundings—they may no longer consistently understand that they're in their own bedroom or living room. That is when you will agonize over having made a promise to keep them in their own home, and your remorse will be followed by a tidal wave of guilt when your loved one's health-care needs finally compel you to break it.

Make a Promise You *Can* Keep

If you shouldn't promise to keep your mom or dad at home, what should you say instead? Give your mom or dad a version of your mirror promise—the promise that you made to yourself—that you will always, always, always take care of them and that you will always make sure they get the best possible care, no matter what they need.

Prepare for Assisted Living

More frequent hospitalizations are often a part of aging, and many older patients transition to a skilled nursing facility (SNF) or a convalescent home after they are released from acute care. Hospital releases can happen abruptly. "Your mom is being discharged today" is not the time to start looking for an assisted-living arrangement. Be prepared and have a few alternative destinations in mind.

If you start to anticipate that placing a parent into a skilled nursing facility may become inevitable, or even likely, do some advance planning. Have an idea of what's available in your community. Get referrals from physicians and from other women who have been through the process. Check reputations and reviews. Above all, make the rounds and visit—see with your own eyes and form your own opinions.

- ## Don't Put Your Children in This Situation

  The one thing you know for sure is that the seesaw *will* tilt again. And you will still be on it. Don't make your children agonize over your care when you are older. Imagine several scenarios for your own health a decade or more down the road and figure out what your preferences are. Explore long-term care insurance coverage. If you can afford it, it will give your kids great peace of mind. If necessary, enlist the help of an estate planner or an eldercare planner. And, yes, you are thinking the unthinkable, but once you've thunk it, it's done, and you will feel *so* much better. So will your kids. Learn from the challenges of caring for your grandparents and parents, and, in this case, don't let history repeat itself.

8

Girls Just Wanna Have Funds

$\mathcal{I}$was eight years old when I started learning about money. My dad was my first teacher. He was the one who paid the bills in our family. Mom stayed out of it, which was probably wise, since Dad is not only a CPA but a bit of a control freak—just like me. I suspect that I got my bossiness from him, and I'm pretty sure it's genetic—there's little doubt that I've passed it down to my daughter, Mollie.

Dad used to sit at our walnut-brown Early American kitchen table, the one with the thin top and a peeling veneer that always felt sticky, and four matching hard, spindle-back chairs. I always wanted to know what he was doing, so I'd sit beside him. In the summertime I sat real still because it hurt to move—my legs always stuck to the seat. As he paid the bills, he'd explain everything as he went along—this is how much money we have, this is how much we owe to the lender for our mortgage, to the bank for the car payment, to the power company to keep the lights on. He always paid the bills on Thursday evening, and it became something of a ritual for the two of us. I may now have Wednesdays with Mom, but back then I had Thursdays with Dad. I never realized how important Thursdays with Dad would be to my future.

My financial education continued after high school. I knew early on that I wanted to open my own shop, so Dad made sure I took business courses in college. I learned about cash flow, profits, and payroll. Nevertheless, when Eddie and I got married, I assumed that he would be responsible for our family finances, just like my dad had been. It took me a little while to figure out that his system was a lot more, well, casual than my dad's. In other words, Eddie pretty much threw the bills into the corner and let 'em pile up there till he got around to writing the checks. (And yes, checks. Our marriage is waaay older than online banking.) Pink is one of my favorite colors, but I soon learned that pink envelopes were not a good thing. Inside them were nastygrams—reminders about bills that were past due. Seeing those pink envelopes was when I took over the checkbook. I still pay all the bills, and I'm anal about it because I can't stand owing people money.

This is a lesson I learned from Dad. Pay all your bills, pay them on time, and, if you can't pay them off in full that month, get them paid off as quickly as you can. Long before I heard it from any financial guru, my dad always preached that there was no better feeling in this world than being without debt.

I realize that my upbringing and my education are not typical. Many in our tribe were raised to believe that talking out loud about the dollars and cents of personal finance was not genteel or lady-like. Our mothers and grandmothers taught us that it was rude or unseemly, like speaking in public about sex, if not worse.

Perhaps you were brought up to think women were not supposed to get involved in household finance, that money was a man's domain. That attitude was common enough back in the day, but it went out with Britney Spears's cutesy pigtails—or it should have. And for the same reason—it was never a good look for you, or for any grown woman.

It's also wrong. Guys are not inherently better at money management than we are. There are no finance genes, and they don't hang out on the Y chromosome. Money savvy isn't male or female—it just is. The more you know about it, the better it will work for you, both now and in the future.

Hope for the Best, Plan for the Worst

Money can make you feel like a failure, but it shouldn't. Nearly all people go through difficult financial times in their lives—the key is keeping your wits about you when it happens. When we're scared, we tend to stop thinking clearly. All those stupid things characters do in horror movies when they're being chased by a werewolf or an abominable snowman or Freddy Krueger—it's the same with financial anxiety. Operating in panic mode can push you into fear-based decisions—more often than not, those are not wise choices. It's far better to face whatever it is head-on, lay out all your potential options, and rationally figure out a workable plan.

I know because it happened to me. I opened Bridals by Lori ten days after I graduated from Columbia College. I started with a generous $40,000 loan from my parents, but I knew from the outset that there would be no more where that came from. I've long since paid them back, but because they believed enough in me to get me started, I've always felt an enormous responsibility to be successful. I still feel today as if I'm standing on their shoulders—their faith in me enabled me to become who I am.

From the beginning I was cautious but deliberate about expansion, and we grew as Atlanta grew. By the late 1990s, we were located in a 7,500-square-foot building that I'd bought, but I could already see that we needed more room. As I began looking around for a bigger space, a three-story building housing a plastic surgery hospital caught my eye. It was 25,000 square feet—twenty-five times the size of the shop I'd started out in two decades earlier. It was in an ideal location, and when its owner got into financial difficulty, it was auctioned off. The winning bid was mine. Relatively speaking, I got a bargain, but it was still a major financial outlay for me—and of course, the building was going to need a lot of work to be transformed from a dull medical facility into the open, airy store of my dreams.

When I purchased it, we were told that renovation would take a year. It took two, and the budget ended up being double what the contractor had originally said it would be. Twice as long and twice as much—toward the end of the renovation process, I was pretty much tapped out.

And then it got worse. Right as we were planning the grand opening, 9/11 happened. On that terrible September morning, we were still crammed into the old store, and all of us had gathered around the television in the break room. We were holding one another up, already numb with horror and disbelief, when the second plane hit the towers. As they collapsed, it felt like the whole world was caving in. In a way, it was—and not just in the way we were seeing on TV.

While our eyes were riveted on the staggering catastrophe in front of us, a customer walked out of the store with a bridal gown—without paying. Can you believe it? Something old, something new, something borrowed, something blue—something stolen? I can't begin to imagine standing in a church before God and your family, taking your vows to be faithful and true, all while wearing your dishonesty for all to see. Vengeance is not mine to take, but I know what God thinks about stealing. I also know that what goes around comes around—and from a direction you'd least expect it.

I went to Bridal Fashion Week in New York that October, less than a month after the terrorist attack. I love New York. Over the years, we've shot several *Say Yes* episodes in Manhattan during that week—it's the one trip Monte and I always look forward to making together. The bridal community is small and close-knit—Bridal Fashion Week is like a reunion, our chance to renew old friendships and make new ones. It's usually such an exciting, festive time. Not that year. Hardly anyone was there, but I felt it was important to attend and show my support, both for our industry and for the city itself. New York was in shock. Fifth Avenue was closed to traffic several times a day for funeral processions for first responders. Much of the city was otherworldly quiet and subdued, and I remember being able to smell the smoking pile from miles away, long before you could see it.

America was still reeling as we moved into our new building. Everyone was dazed and all but frozen in place as we waited to see what was going to happen. Was this just the first of many attacks? Were we going to war? People were scared to fly, but they were also scared to make major decisions, including the commitment to get married.

That stolen gown turned out to be an omen for trouble ahead. There was so much fear and uncertainty that the wedding business simply imploded, just like the towers. Caterers, bakers, florists—no one in the business was receiving orders. Everything just stopped.

Gown sales plummeted to zero. I no longer had to worry about some-one shoplifting a gown—our beautiful new store, all three floors of it, was empty. There are peaks and valleys in every business cycle, but this was the Grand Canyon, and we were at the bottom of it. It's still the scariest time in retail that I've ever been through.

Our family was already financially stretched. Eddie and I were paying two private-school tuitions, one for college, one for high school, and we were still facing major outlays on the renovations. Cash flow quickly became a serious problem. I didn't know from one week to the next whether I could make payroll at the shop—for a while, it looked like we might lose everything. I started to wonder if the building itself somehow had a hex on it. The prior occupant was a plastic surgeon who'd gone bankrupt, and I remembered that there had been a Realtor in there who'd gone belly-up as well. Did that mean I was next?

Nope. Not this girl. I was determined that this shop, this dream of mine, was not going under. I owed that to my parents, and I owed it to myself. Eddie and I sat down and talked out our options, but giving up was never on the table. We ended up taking out a second mortgage on our home and putting that money into Bridals by Lori. We had to, just to stay afloat. We did so with the understanding that we were making a double-or-nothing bet: if there was war or deep financial recession, and it turned out that our customers were gone permanently, we'd have lost not just the building but our home as well. Eventually business bounced back—it always does, if you can afford to wait out the bad times.

And that's the moral of this story: the bottom can drop out, even if you've taken what seems like a prudent risk, even if you've tried to do everything right. And that's why you've got to have a backup system in place. If Eddie and I hadn't had equity in our home to borrow on, Bridals by Lori might have been another 9/11 casualty.

Personal Financial Literacy

I'm guessing you don't own a bridal shop, but the principle holds just as true for your personal finances as it does for my business. When things are going well, that's the time to make plans for the inevitable rainy day—you never know when it's going to come down in buckets.

Making those plans is hard if you aren't familiar with money management, but that's a life skill that you should have in your arsenal. To me, literacy and money competence—financial literacy—are very similar. If you're a Rockefeller or a DuPont or a Kardashian, you can afford to hire people to manage your money. But what happens if your family is not wealthy? What happens if you've always left all of those financial decisions to your spouse and he's no longer able to make them? What happens if he's no longer your spouse?

Having a husband is not the same as having a financial plan—even if he's prudent about handling money. Going into this next phase of life, you're going to need more than a mate, and I say this based on statistics, not on any husband in particular. (Love you, Eddie!) According to a recent study spearheaded by George Washington University, nine of every ten women will eventually find themselves responsible for their own finances.[1] Most end up in this position as a result of divorce or widowhood, and when they're suddenly thrust into that responsibility, many are caught flat-footed by how much they don't know. Stepping into your big-girl panties is never easy, but it's super hard if you have to hit the ground running and jump into them both feet at once.

It's common for women in our tribe to admit that they know nothing about finance. What's disappointing is how many are still disinclined to learn. I hear women say, "I'm just not good with money," as if that's an incurable, permanent condition, like herpes. Why would you be okay with remaining deliberately ignorant about something so important? Would you be content with being illiterate forever, blowing it off because you've decided that you're "not good at reading"?

We're going to work on that, starting now.

But what if math scares you? I can tell that a lot of you are nodding your heads. Your fears might be a holdover from childhood—time was when girls in school were not expected to excel in math. Take a deep breath—you've got this! Being comfortable handling finances is a means to an end. Managing your money is less about math and numbers and more about having the confidence and the freedom to live life the way you envision.

If you've never been involved in your finances, as you head into this next stage of life, you can't afford to be ignorant anymore. Why? For sheer self-defense, if nothing else. In general, women earn less than men over the course of our working lives, so being prudent about managing what we have is essential. Because we tend to marry men slightly older than we are, and because our life expectancy is longer, we're also going to have to know how to make those dollars last longer and stretch a little further when we're on our own.

None of this is a big secret. The people in those TV commercials trying to sell us money management services know all about it, but those ads represent just the most high-profile companies in the business. The financial advice industry is gigantic, and sadly, not all of it is on the level. Unscrupulous individuals make a very good living playing to our insecurities and our naivete as we get older. They understand how vulnerable women can be, and they know easy prey when they see it. They'd like nothing better than to eat the rest of your cookie, and they have no compunctions about leaving you without even a morsel. Beyond a doubt, in this field what you don't know *can* hurt you.

So let's talk about financial literacy—what every woman needs to know. But as we begin, let's understand that there is no way to be comprehensive in just one chapter. My plan is to cover some of the basics and highlight a few of the most important aspects. To point you in the right direction, I'm going to suggest some questions you need to pose—to your spouse, to your children, and, most of all, to yourself. Getting the answers will guide you to a brighter financial future—and a bigger, better cookie, with plenty of chocolate chips and extra frosting—in this next phase of your life. I hope that rather than being intimidated by money management, you'll be empowered by it instead.

Your Financial Selfie

If you want to know where you're going and how to get there, the first step is knowing where you are—and many of us don't have a clue. To do that, take a look at both sides of your financial status, what businesses would call a balance sheet. Start with your liabilities—the monthly bills that have to be paid, and long-term debt obligations, including mortgages and other loans. Then move on to your assets—your income and what you own—not just home and auto but also cash on hand; an emergency fund, if you have one (and you should); plus stocks, bonds, pensions, insurance policies, and retirement accounts.

You may also have bought or inherited some heirloom collectibles. Show of hands, you antique hunters and flea marketeers—you know who you are. Your great-grandpa's gold retirement watch from the railroad and that Tiffany sterling tea set you inherited from Aunt Josephine most assuredly count as assets (have you insured them?), but some pop-culture items might be valuable as well. *Not* your daughter's Beanie Babies, but if you have vintage Barbie dolls, or 1950s metal lunchboxes that don't smell like bologna sandwiches, or your dad's Superman comic books—in great condition—they could be worth more than you think.

When you subtract your liabilities from your assets, you'll get a picture of your net worth—a financial snapshot at a moment in time. If the difference is tiny, or if there's a minus sign in front of the balance, this may be the point at which many of you will be tempted to stop reading and pull the covers over your head. That's not the right response. Whatever your current status is, it's not going to get better if you hide from it. Running away from the problem doesn't qualify as a financial strategy. This is your starting point. Now it's time to take steps to put yourself on track to improve.

While you're preparing your snapshot, take a few minutes to check your credit report. Make sure there aren't any debts showing up on there that you didn't know about (perhaps a bill that went to collection after an ex left it unpaid) or, worse yet, any incorrect information that could affect your creditworthiness. Some of you may believe that checking your credit score affects your credit rating, but in general that's not the case. Being aware of your rating and checking it regularly will help you figure out how to boost your score. Consumer credit reporting companies offer ways for you to check your rating, but many lenders and credit card companies offer this service as well. It may appear on your monthly statement, or it may be accessible online, through the institution's website.

Retain the Services of a Financial Planner

Once you have an idea of your current situation, it's time to get some professional advice. If you have concerns about how much you don't know or fears about outliving your money, a financial planner is a must. In a way, a good financial planner is just like a good dentist or good hairstylist. Not only do they have to be skilled at their profession, but they must also be in sync with you on a personal level. You must trust that they have the best interest of your teeth or your hair or your money at heart, and it should never make you nervous to go see them.

Eddie and I first connected with a financial adviser while Mollie and Cory were in college. We didn't have a lot, but we wanted to protect what we had. He looked over our assets and announced, "Well, you're cash poor."

"No kidding," I said. "We barely survived the retail slump after 9/11. Other than our home, our primary assets are the Bridals by Lori building and anything in it that's on a hanger. We've been putting everything we make back into the business."

"I strongly suggest that you and Eddie each take out a major life insurance policy," he said. "If something were to happen to you, your children would have to pay the taxes because of your business. Having insurance will give you peace of mind."

We followed his recommendation, and within just a few years, we were very glad we did. The year 2012 was the year I got cancer, but it was also the year Eddie got cancer too. We are now cancer-free, but as cancer survivors, we're no longer as "insurable" as we'd been before. There's no way we could qualify today for the amount of coverage we took out back then. Needless to say, we make sure those premiums are always paid on time.

We received excellent advice from our financial planner, but your planner may suggest different priorities for you. In fact, that's likely—and that's exactly the point. We received great guidance for who we were and what we needed at that time in our lives—not one-size-fits-all advice that could have been given to anyone.

How do you find a financial planner? Make sure you are looking for the right kind of person—seek out someone qualified to coordinate all aspects of your financial life, and who can orchestrate those resources toward helping you reach your goals. Be aware that there are also financial advisers who focus mainly or even exclusively on investments. My guess is, for most of you, that's not the kind of adviser you need.

Before making a commitment to work with an adviser, use caution. Some of them receive hefty commissions and earn them by funneling your cash toward the companies whose products—mutual funds, real estate investment trusts—they represent. An independent financial adviser may cost you more out of pocket than an adviser who is looking to shepherd your money into these investment opportunities, but as in any field, if you want to know who somebody works for, look at who signs their paycheck. Be certain that you have a financial adviser who is paid to work on behalf of your money, not to steer it in a particular direction to someone else.

By all means, get referrals for financial planners from friends, but don't stop there—check them out online, and check them out for yourself. One adviser may have been commended to you because she's a member of your church, and that nice lady in your book club may have suggested a young man who turns out to be her nephew. Even if they're competent, are they a good fit for your needs?

If you keep asking around and are diligent enough, the same names may start to pop up from different corners of your social universe—these are your leading candidates. Think of it like hiring a new employee or retaining a skilled craftsman to make improvements on your home—meet with prospective financial advisers in person, and meet with more than one. Have a list of questions you'd like to ask that are particular to your situation. If you can, try to ask all of them the same questions, and then compare their responses.

Check to make sure that your financial planner has excellent credentials. Don't just look for a plaque on the wall, y'all—all credentials are not created equal. If you see a plaque that reads CFP—Certified Financial Planner—that's a good thing. The CFP designation is conferred by the Center for Financial Planning, which is a well-regarded institution. That plaque means that the Center is vouching for an individual who has taken their coursework, passed a rigorous exam, and meets both experience and ethics criteria. For those who want to focus more narrowly on retirement planning, these other designations were found reputable by the *Wall Street Journal*: Retirement Income Certified Professional (RICP), sponsored by the American College of Financial Services, and Certified Retirement Counselor (CRC), offered through the International Foundation for Retirement Education.

Feeling comfortable with your financial planner is essential. First, they should be accessible. If you have questions, you should be able to pick up the phone and have a conversation from time to time without booking an appointment weeks or months in advance. Also, you should never get the feeling that they're talking down to you or humoring you. They should both educate and empower you at the same time. Most importantly, there should be no expectation that you completely surrender your financial future to them, then take a step back and let them run it.

Some advisers charge by the hour, others by the plan; either way, I believe that you'll find it money well spent. When the amount you save, or the amount you add to your future nest egg—and to your present peace of mind—exceeds what you've paid for that advice, I'd consider that an investment, not an expense, wouldn't you?

Less Shopping = More Savings

With the help of your planner, it's now time to look into your future. Do you like what you see? Project your current financial snapshot forward. How will your income change over time? What will happen with your expenditures? Will you have enough resources to comfortably retire, or can you see a gap forming in the future? Now is the time to maximize your future potential, which may entail some belt-tightening on what you're now spending.

How do you balance the ins and outs? How do you plan for the future? Start with a realistic budgeting plan that not only helps you manage your money today but also puts aside savings for tomorrow.

You can find dozens of online budgeting apps to choose from. Many of them can be linked directly to your banking program and will categorize your expenditures automatically. Several, including one called Mint (mint.com), will generate a pie chart so you can see at a glance how you are spending your money. In addition to tracking income and expenditures, Mint will also monitor your credit score and your investments.

Online and radio financial adviser Dave Ramsey has authored a suite of financial advice books. His website, www.daveramsey.com, also offers budgeting and retirement planning advice.

The AARP (American Association of Retired Persons) website is another good place to begin. Their program called Finances 50+ SM (which stands for Smart Money) teaches budgeting and goal setting, asset management, and taking control of your own financial future. It includes worksheets on savings, goal setting, and other financial essentials.[2]

The National Endowment for Financial Education can also help you get off on the right foot. Topics include spending and saving (a.k.a. budgeting), debt and credit management, and investing.[3]

Ditch the Debt

Some in our tribe feel mired in bills—credit card and other debt that they can't seem to get rid of. Those kinds of obligations drag you down. They take a toll not just on your finances but on your physical and emotional health as well. Time for a strategy to get debt-free. There are many approaches to doing this—your financial planner may have an approach you prefer—but all of them involve developing a clear-eyed, purposeful strategy for paying down those big balances.

Financial guru Dave Ramsey suggests one technique that seems to work for many people. He calls it the "debt snowball," and its simplicity has a lot going for it. Make a list of all of your debts and categorize them from smallest to largest. The debt at the top—the smallest—is Target #1. As you make minimum payments (just enough to stay current) on everything from #2 down, make payments as large as you can on #1 to pay it off as quickly as possible. Once you've dispatched Target #1, take the funds you'd dedicated to paying that off and put them toward Target #2. Repeat as necessary till it's all gone.[4]

Starting with the smallest debt first may sound counterintuitive, but the feeling of satisfaction that comes with paying off a credit card generates momentum—the snowball—which is a great incentive to keep going. Other approaches entail the same kinds of listings but use a different priority system. Strategies to pay off the largest amount first or to start with the debt that has the biggest interest percentage are also common. The important thing is to have a strategy and stick to it.

Cut Back on Your Shoe Collection

Do you treat yourself to a venti no-whip no-foam latte—daily—because you "deserve" it? Does your favorite barista know your order by heart? Does she greet you by name when you walk in the door? If so, I suspect that your local coffee emporium—the one whose logo is a green-and-white mermaid with a star in her crown—is getting too many of your bucks.

Lattes have become emblematic of financial irresponsibility, and in some ways it's a bad rap. I'm not suggesting that cutting them out is the key to a comfortable retirement, but I *am* suggesting that there is probably money hemorrhaging from your budget due to careless spending.

We all have our little luxuries, the discretionary expenses that we are reluctant to cut. Those indulgences may look like lattes, like concert tickets, or like those open-toed, teal suede booties you couldn't resist (don't go there—if you haven't already worn them, take them back!). Those purchases may not seem so extravagant one by one, but they add up. Sometimes these splurges are for ourselves, but often they're for others. Do you have grandchildren you love to spoil? Has that come to mean never walking through the door empty-handed? This is me, or at least it had been, till now. I'm a giver, and I tend to overdo it. I love planning huge family trips and giving over-the-top gifts to my grandchildren. You may think you can afford this in the here and now, but be aware that your generosity may come at the expense of your future.

Avoid getting into the position where your giving comes to be expected. You'll find that even though you don't always bring the big gift or pick up the tab, your family members will still love you just for your own wonderful self. (And if becoming less generous creates tension or causes a rift, that should tell you something too.) Shift your mindset—this is your time and your season. How much of your cookie can you really afford to give away?

While you're hunting for ways to be more prudent about expenses, also be on the lookout for money you might be leaving on the table. Are you sure you're taking advantage of every benefit you're entitled to? Could there be an annuity you've forgotten about? Are there assets of an ex-spouse that are legally half yours? Find out whether some of what should be your money is slipping through your fingers.

Reverse Mortgage?

If it looks like you might come up short of the amount of money you'd like to have to live comfortably, tapping the equity in your home by taking out a reverse mortgage may look tempting. Is this a good idea? Maybe yes, maybe no.

The good news is that you would no longer have to make a monthly mortgage payment, which would give you some relief. You'd also have some cash to tap into. That money could be disbursed in a number of ways—as a lump sum, as a monthly payment, as a line of credit, or as some combination of the three.

The bad news is that, month by month, the interest you owe will be tacked on to the balance of the mortgage. If you remain in your home long enough, the total amount could eventually exceed the value of the property itself, especially in geographic areas of the country where housing prices are rising slowly or, worse yet, declining. In that case, if you'd been hoping to leave your home to your children, there might be nothing left.

Your bank or other mortgage holder also expects you to remain current on your homeowner's insurance and property tax payments, which continue to be your responsibility. You are also required to keep your home in good repair. Failure to live up to these obligations could result in foreclosure.

Taking out a reverse mortgage is a big decision. Before committing to one, consult with your financial planner and make sure you fully understand the implications of how it works. This is a very risky proposition. Ask your planner whether there are other ways to achieve the same or similar results with fewer downsides. It may also be time to ask a different and perhaps harder question: In the long run, can you really afford to remain in your home, and would downsizing into a smaller house or condo be a better solution?

Think Before You Help

In addition to indulging your grandchildren, you may also be shouldering some or all of the costs of caring for family members who are unwell. Those expenditures can eat a large hole in even the most comfortable nest egg. Women constitute two-thirds of all family caregivers. Providing free care not only isn't free, but it has a price all its own.

Beyond the out-of-pocket outlays for health-care items such as prescriptions and over-the-counter medications, caregivers also pay indirectly, and those costs continue to adversely affect them long into the years ahead. Women who care for aging parents or an ailing spouse are financially surrendering part of their own future. This comes in the form of lost income from days, months, or even years of not working, or working less than full-time, or accepting a lower wage or salary as the tradeoff for more flexible hours. These sacrifices not only shrink take-home pay but also reduce the size of 401(k) contributions they can make (and that can be matched by an employer), as well as the dollar amount of Social Security benefits they ultimately receive.

If you find yourself in this position, there are no easy answers, but do know that there are women just like you all over this country who have nothing saved for their retirement because they cared for someone they loved who got sick. If you have siblings, this is not a burden that you should bear alone. Bring them into the equation—be prepared to tell them how much this effort is costing you and how they can contribute. If caring for an elder parent or an ailing spouse is part of your present sphere of responsibility, or if it's a need you can anticipate in the future, be sure to raise the issue with your financial adviser.

The Time Is Now

If you've avoided financial planning, or if you handed off the responsibility for it to your husband years ago, it's time for you to take back your power. Make the effort to get involved and be prepared to be persistent. Don't get cowed by the jargon or by the magnitude of what you have to learn. Take it step-by-step. There's no better time to take control of your own financial future—there's always something you can do.

WHAT'S NEXT
Girlfriends' Guide

- ### Find a Financial Planner

  Don't make the mistake of thinking that you have to be wealthy to have a financial planner—women who face significant financial challenges need one the most. Connect with someone in your community who can help you understand your current financial picture and guide you toward what you want that picture to look like in the future.

  Know the terms going in. When you ask how they are compensated for their advice to you, they should provide you with a clear, unambiguous answer. You should have an explicit, signed contract that stipulates exactly what they're going to do for you, what financial plans and other work products they will produce, and how those plans will be implemented. Will they just lay out the plan and leave the execution to you, or will they be hands-on in putting it into practice?

- ### Be on the Lookout for Additional Sources of Income

  Cutting costs will bring you more resources for the future, but so will added revenue. If retirement doesn't sound appealing—or affordable—are there jobs or entrepreneurial opportunities that might appeal to you? If there are assets you are keeping for sentimental reasons, would you be financially more at ease facing the future if you sold them off?

- **Face What Scares You**

  For many women our age, it's the prospect of outliving our money. If you have a retirement plan, great—monitor it with your financial planner.

- **Up Your Financial Literacy by Finding Out the Answers to These Questions:**

  » How much do you owe on your mortgage? What rate of interest are you paying? Is it fixed or adjustable?

  » How much is your home worth? Do you know how much you pay in property tax?

  » How much do you owe on your car? How many years till it's paid off?

  » How much do you pay monthly in utilities—heating, air-conditioning, electricity, water? How much does the amount fluctuate from one season to another?

  » What is your monthly food bill? How much is from purchases at the supermarket? How much is from takeout and dining out?

  » How much do you pay for your cell phone? Cable TV? Internet access?

  » How much do you pay for a health club membership? Do you use it?

» Do you carry life insurance? How much? Who is the beneficiary?

- Plan for the Future

» Do you have a pension? Does your spouse have a pension? Does a *former* spouse have a pension, and are you legally entitled to some of it?

» Who's managing that pension account, and how do you get access to it if you need it?

» If you were to be widowed, do you know how to claim the survivor benefits or pension benefits to which you are entitled?

» You may soon be entitled to receive a monthly payment from Social Security, if you aren't getting one already. Do you know how much it will be? Do you want to take it at age sixty-two? Sixty-five? Seventy? What are the short-term and long-term implications of each of those choices?

» How much is your husband's Social Security benefit? Is it bigger than your own? If he were to pass away, do you know how to claim it instead of yours?

» Did you know that if you are over the age of sixty-two, were married for more than ten years, and have not remarried, you may have a claim to your ex's Social

Security benefit—even if he's remarried? Collecting it will not affect what he receives. This is yet another topic to discuss with your financial planner.

- ## Take a Deep Breath and Just Start

Educate yourself. Don't be so embarrassed by your lack of information that you become immobilized. It's never too late to take control of your future—and your present. If you can't bring yourself to seek help in person quite yet, you can start by learning online. Don't procrastinate, because not planning actually *is* a plan—it means that your future is being determined by someone else who may not have your best interests at heart.

One good place to start is at WISER—the Women's Institute for a Secure Retirement. WISER is a nonprofit organization that's been around for almost a quarter century and is focused on education that will improve the long-range financial quality of life for women. They have created a variety of informational materials for women that explain in simple terms the ins and outs of Social Security, pensions, savings, and investments. Perhaps most importantly, they have made a point to focus on women who do not have a lot of background in financial matters and who are most at risk for poverty in old age.[5]

Always remember, girls just wanna have funds!

9

BFF = Better Find Friends

Friends are chosen family. I don't share DNA with any of them, but I'm so incredibly blessed that these people are part of my clan. First and foremost, there's Monte Durham. He and I have been besties for twenty years, ever since I saw him during Bridal Fashion Week in New York. When we first met, Monte was the new image director for a bridal designer whose gowns I carried. The designer had taken the penthouse suite at the Waldorf Astoria to premiere her new collection, and I arrived for the fashion show.

As he welcomed me to the suite, Monte made an indelible first impression. His hair was in a ponytail at the nape of his neck, and he was wearing a perfectly tailored black linen Dolce & Gabbana Nehru jacket with six muted brass buttons, and a statement necklace with a jade cross. Style, charm, and charisma oozed out of every pore. I looked over at him and thought, *Who is that? Is he a model or movie star?* Whoever he was, I knew he was special.

When Monte introduced himself and asked me to take my seat, I told him, "You know what? I'm hosting a fashion show in my store next week, and you're going to be there for it." That was a tad bossy of me, I know, but I was instantly drawn to him in a way that was absolutely compelling.

I don't know that he was drawn to me in quite the same way. Actually, I do—and he wasn't—at least not at that particular moment. Years later, he told me that as soon as I'd said that, he'd stormed into the back, where the models were getting ready, and confronted the designer. "Who's that bossy blonde out there?" he asked. "I thought you and I had an understanding that I get to make my own schedule, but she just informed me that I'd be going to Atlanta next week!"

The designer let Monte know that I was one of their top accounts and suggested that for the sake of his job security, he should consider being nice to me. And, yes, he was at Bridals by Lori the following week. He was a bit withdrawn at the beginning, but then I took him to dinner because I just *knew* he was going to be my best friend. It didn't take long for us to realize that we were both smart alecks. We laughed and laughed—we hit it off completely. We realized at that dinner that we had so much in common—our love of fashion, history, china, family, and the bridal industry above all.

Since then, Monte has been an integral part of my life and the lives of my family members. When TLC called, I knew that I couldn't do *Say Yes to the Dress: Atlanta* without him. He lives most of the year in the DC area, but when I told him about shooting the pilot, he was on the first plane down here. He's my heart twin. We say the same thing at the same time, and we finish each other's sentences—it's as if we came out of the same egg. We also seem to be going through all of life's trials and tribulations in the same time frame—including struggling to help our parents as they get older. We're so thankful that we can share our feelings and our experiences with each other.

When he and Jack got married, I was the bridesmaid at the wedding, and Eddie was best man. Both of us were thrilled and honored to be part of their ceremony. For their special day, I wanted to show Monte that I loved him enough to make the ultimate sacrifice. Because he adores Jackie O, I wore a pillbox hat—even though I knew that perching that thing on my head would give me a migraine—even though I knew that it made me look like a bellhop.

Being Monte's friend brings me so much joy, love, and support every day, but most importantly, our closeness is a living, breathing reminder of the single most important lesson about friendship: not to have any preconceived notions about who can be your friend. Friendship is where you find it and what you make of it. A true friend can be found anywhere and at any time. Your friend doesn't have to be female or your age or your faith or anything like you at all.

Think of how many examples of powerful but unlikely friendships there are in the Bible. There's Ruth and Naomi, of course, but also consider the collection of people who were Jesus' friends and closest companions—a few fishermen, a tax collector, a woman of questionable virtue. Consider how different they were from him and from one another. They were anything but perfect people, but he loved them for who they were and where they were in their lives. And that's the example we all should follow.

A friend is someone who's got your back in every situation. A friend is your 4:00 a.m. phone call. Whether you're happy or sad or sick—or need bail money—your friend is the one person you *know* will pick up at that dismal hour, or whenever your number pops up on their cell phone screen. Monte certainly has been that lifeline for me. He and I talk three or more times a day, even if we're time zones apart.

I know I can call him at any time of day or night—and I do. He feels the same way. We're there 100 percent for each other, and we both know it.

He is also the godfather to Mollie's two girls, and before that, he was totally hands-on in planning her wedding to Jason. Mollie and Monte have always hit it off. Both are Virgos, and in many ways, he understands her better than I do. The two of them have long since established their own special bond—he's not just my friend but is a central figure in her life as well. Monte was also influential in Cory and Becca's wedding planning process. He and Jack are members of our family, and they're included in all aspect of our lives, from baptisms to babies and everything in between.

Following my mastectomy, Monte was right there when I needed him most. Having been off for several months, I was getting ready to come back to work, but post-op lymphedema, which is common after breast cancer surgery, had really puffed up my arms, my right arm in particular. This was a major wardrobe problem. We were about to start filming new episodes of *Say Yes to the Dress: Atlanta*, but every jacket I owned fit me like a sausage casing.

As soon as I told Monte about it, he didn't hesitate. "You're going shopping," he announced. He didn't ask me if I wanted to go. He made it clear that I didn't have a choice. In that grand and marvelous way of his that straddles the border between regal and imperious, Monte pretty much threw me into the car and said, "You're going."

Because I still didn't have much range of motion in my arms, trying on jackets was physically difficult. This sweet, thoughtful man—my best friend—gently helped ease my swollen limbs into jacket after jacket. Or tried to—with many of them, I got stuck in the sleeves long before I could see my fingertips. Wriggling out of them was almost impossible—Monte had to pretty much peel them off me. It was arduous, painful, and frustrating, and if he hadn't been there with me, I know I would have given up in tears. With Monte's assistance and persistence, I ended up with three Armani sweater jackets—because they're knitted, they could stretch to accommodate my arms, and they were even on sale. I still have those jackets in my closet. That's what friends do. Whether you need a pat on the back or a kick in the pants—or both—they're there with whatever it takes.

Because so much of my life revolves around the store, many of my dearest friends are part of the Bridals by Lori family and the *Say Yes to the Dress: Atlanta* cast. I'm especially close with Robin Gibbs, Flori Watters, and Megan LaMonica since they've been there with me from the beginning of the *Say Yes* journey, almost ten years ago. We've been through countless major life moments together—from health struggles, to loss of family members, to growing children, to weddings, to new babies. What a ride! These women are not only my managers but dear friends as well. There are also many other strong women in the store. They're family, and I'm thankful for all of them.

We carried designer Judd Waddell's elegant gowns at Bridals by Lori for many years, until he decided to leave the bridal industry and return to work for famed designer Carolina Herrera. I've known Judd for countless years. When I found out I had breast cancer, I knew I had to tell him, but I sure didn't want to. His mother had it, too, and he'd already told me that she wasn't doing well. I worried that telling Judd about my diagnosis would add to his burden of worry and sorrow, but I didn't want him to hear about it from someone else either. In my lighthearted way, I sent him a text—"Hey Judd, just wanted to let you know that I've got breast cancer . . ."

Delivering that kind of news in a text message—what was I thinking? I'd barely hit Send when my phone rang. It was Judd, of course, encouraging me to fight and assuring me that I was going to get through it.

Not all my friends were that supportive. After my mastectomy, some of them had trouble making eye contact with me—they'd look at my forehead or at the wall behind me. To me, that meant they were convinced that either breast cancer was contagious, or that I wasn't going to make it. I didn't want anyone feeling sorry for me, and I needed strength, not sympathy. Look me in the eye. That's what a real friend does.

Friends share the load—whatever challenge you're facing, they let you know that they're right there beside you. A few months later Judd was in Atlanta doing a trunk show at the shop—by this time, his mom had passed away. I was in my office when he came in to see me. "I have something for you," he said. Then he presented me with the most beautiful David Yurman bracelet I've ever seen—Judd knew I love David Yurman.

"This was my mother's," he said simply. "I bought it for her, and now I want you to have it. She didn't win this fight, but you're going to." Then we hugged and just sobbed on each other. It was a gut-wrenching sob, and it still feels so raw to tell the story.

Friends are people you can cry on, for sure. After my surgery the steroids and other drugs I needed to take made me a wreck, inside and out. I looked and felt awful, and my self-esteem was in the dumpster sub-basement. The meds also messed with my emotions—I cried at everything and nothing. When designer Lázaro Pérez came to Atlanta, I blubbered like crazy at him. "Lázaro, I'm going to be giving all these speeches about breast cancer awareness, and I'm so bloated I look like a balloon animal. Nothing fits. What am I going to wear?"

"Don't even think about it," he said. "Leave it to me."

He propelled me into one of our dressing rooms and told me to undress. I did—didn't think twice about it, even though there was no hiding my neon purple surgical scars. Then he pulled one of those yellow dressmaker's tapes out of his pocket and started taking all my measurements. He quickly drew up sketches of the two dresses he planned to make for me—I have those treasured drawings framed and hanging in my office. The dresses themselves arrived on my doorstep in record time. They were gorgeous, of course, and I felt so proud—and so loved—as I gave my speeches while wearing them. Friends are essential to your physical and emotional well-being. They can rescue you from your darkest moments and turn them into some of your brightest days ever.

Say No to Loneliness

Going into this new phase of your life, friends should be more important than ever, but I know that a lot of us find ourselves lonely and adrift instead. The kids are gone, the nest is empty, and maybe you're working part-time or not at all. Or perhaps you were burned or let down in the past by women you thought were your friends, so you've shied away from forming meaningful friendships. One way or another, you're suddenly spending a lot more time by yourself than you used to.

That's not healthy, girls. For starters, loneliness can take a giant bite out of your cookie. As one researcher put it, "Loneliness acts as a fertilizer for other diseases."[1] Excess solitude is linked to lots of illnesses, both mental and physical, including heart disease, depression, hypertension, anxiety, alcohol and substance abuse, and dementia.[2] Simply put, lonely people die sooner—medical science has found that loneliness is as bad for your health as smoking fifteen cigarettes a day.[3]

Among those especially vulnerable to the adverse effects of loneliness are those who are newly retired, those who have recently become separated from children, friends, or family, and those coping with the death of a spouse or partner.[4]

In other words, *US*.

Friends, BFFs, and Acquaintances

The converse is also true—research has documented a positive feedback loop between health—physical, mental, and emotional—and connection to family and friends.[5] But what if your best friend *is* family? What if he's your husband? That's a good thing, right?

I hear it from brides every day at the shop—"I'm so happy to be marrying my best friend." At this stage of life, some of you may not be lonely, at least not exactly, but perhaps you've started spending almost all your time with your spouse.

Eddie and I were best friends at our wedding decades ago, but no marriage can survive if all you've got is each other. We've already talked about how too much togetherness is bad for your relationship as a couple, but I want to emphasize that it's also bad for you as an individual. Eddie and I are still BFFs today, but Eddie's not enough for me—no husband is, for any of us.

You *need* girlfriends, y'all. You really do. Otherwise, who is going to commiserate with you about all the weird things your husband does? Who's going to take the download when you absolutely have to rant about that strange brand of toothpaste he bought—by the *case*? Or the outfit he ordered for you from Amazon Prime the day before your anniversary—in the wrong size? And who could I tell about the time Eddie wrapped up the free shoes he got from the buy-one-get-one-free sale just in time for my birthday? The issue with that one was that he left the FREE sticker on the box. Oops.

Two dear girlfriends are Cathy and Lillian. We connected over bikes, baseball games, and swing sets in our old neighborhood when Mollie and Cory were young. These friendships have stood the test of time, and we've been there for one another through all of life's ups and downs. We've laughed and cried, and even though we all moved away from that neighborhood, our friendship has remained special. No matter the time of day or night, we're all only a phone call away.

If you've been feeling a bit cut off, maybe you've tried to compensate for lack of close friendships with online relationships—the Internet makes it easy to accumulate Facebook friends. Staying in touch with those friends, who often don't live nearby, may give you a feeling of connection, but they're not the people you can count on in an emergency. They probably think of you the same way. If one of your Facebook friends were to call you in a crisis, would you drop everything to help them? Would you be their 4:00 a.m. phone call?

Make no mistake, you want these folks in your social circle, but I suggest that you push away from the computer screen and focus more on building meaningful face-to-face friendships. Unfortunately, that's a lot harder than it used to be. There's a story about a small village where the women used to gather at the river to wash their clothes. After they all got washing machines, they became depressed. No one understood why, at least at first, but eventually the women figured it out. Although the washers saved them a lot of physical labor, doing the laundry at home meant that they were spending less time with their friends. As a result, they felt lonely and miserable. In its own way, their sense of loss was quite similar to bereavement or grief.[6]

So many of our modern innovations and conveniences—ordering takeout, shopping on Amazon, the drive-thru line at the bank or pharmacy, even headphones—are just like those washing machines.

They tend to keep us isolated, at arm's length from social interaction. As a result, we mourn our lack of connection with others.

Reconnect and Revive Old Friendships

I have a few friends I've known since childhood, and others from college—Brilla, Nancy, Amy, Julie, and Kim. We try to keep in touch through texts and phone calls, but we're now spread all over the map, and I learned about how easily the opportunity to reconnect can slip away. I had one dear friend who had been in my wedding—super sweet girl, but we hadn't spoken in several years. I looked her up, hoping to renew our friendship, but when I googled her name, I learned that she'd died of ovarian cancer. I was shocked and heartbroken, of course. Since then, I've become close with her daughters. Becoming a mentor or a surrogate mom is a great way to expand your friendship circle, and I'm happy to call these young women friends, but I still kick myself for missing my chance to reconnect with their amazing mom, Libby.

If you've attended a high school or college reunion in the hope of rekindling old friendships, you may have been surprised by how much some folks have changed. You also may have found yourself clicking with someone you'd least expect, perhaps even a classmate you barely knew back in the day. I suggest that you follow up on the new connection you've made.

I don't have much expectation that I'm ever going to establish a warm friendship with the mean girl who pushed me down a full flight of stairs in junior high after I made the cheerleading squad. On the other hand, I sure want to talk more with the girl who lived next door to me in the dorm when I was a college freshman. I didn't know her well—nobody did, I suspect—but that political science major who kept to herself and studied constantly is now a senior partner in one of the best law firms in the city. Or the sweet, quiet girl in high school who studied a lot and is now the CEO of a Fortune 500 company. I'd love to tell her just how proud I am of her now. That's another key to friendship—accept and celebrate people as they grow and evolve.

While some relationships deepen, others fade, and some simply wither away. Often it's geography that's to blame for a friendship that's cooled, but relationships can also atrophy from neglect. We all have people in our pasts who we were once close to, but now they've become just someone we used to know—a hazy face, a name, a phone number, and an e-mail address in our list of contacts. If you have old friendships that aren't as close as they once were, you can still breathe new life into them. It won't happen, of course, unless you make the first move, so pick up the phone or send that e-mail. When you do, skip the vague platitudes about wanting to get together. Be specific about making a date—propose a few alternative dates and times, and suggest they choose one of them.

Turn Acquaintances into Friends

If the idea of rekindling a relationship that's been dormant for a while strikes you as awkward, I'm willing to bet that you have more friends-in-waiting than you think you do. Consider generating closer friendships with people who may be acquaintances now. Think about the people you're always happy to see as you go about your daily routine, whether it's a work associate, a neighbor, or that bookstore clerk who remembers what you like to read and always has great new suggestions for you.

Pets are a great way to build a connection. Grab coffee with the smiling face you always see at the dog park—the one whose golden retriever loves your chocolate Lab. Have a real conversation with the woman who walks her bichon frise past your house every day. In my neighborhood, that woman is me! My dear little Chloe and I go walking often, and she has really helped me connect with people who live nearby.

Other hobbies and activities bring people together as well. Some churches have small groups. You may be nervous about attending a weekly gathering for the first time, but once you've been welcomed with open arms, you'll find it easier to return. These connections are our lifeblood, both in friendship and in faith.

Even a relatively solitary pursuit like gardening can help you build connections. A lot of us tend gardens in our backyards, but I have one friend who makes a point of gardening in front of her house so she gets to chat with all the people who stop as they're going by. And there's nothing like ringing your neighbor's doorbell with the offering of a bouquet or some of your best homegrown tomatoes to start a conversation.

With a little nurturing, these friendships can grow and become more meaningful, but you've got to make the effort. Be the one who makes the first move. If the same woman with the great sense of humor always has the bike next to yours in spin class, introduce yourself, then suggest going out for a bite when class is over.

See People

What if this is tremendously difficult for you to do? What if you're so shy that you break out in a cold sweat just thinking about it?

Then you're just like me. You may find it hard to believe, but I'm an introvert. I'm not shy at the store—as soon as I walk in the door, I know it's my job to make my customers feel welcome. I'm super outgoing there, but that's because I'm on my own turf. Outside the shop, and when the camera stops rolling, I have insecurities like everyone else. On Sundays Eddie and I attend an 8:30 church service. I love going, but do you know what I dread from the bottom of my soul every week? That moment when our pastor asks us to turn around and introduce ourselves to the people in the pew behind us. Eddie's fine, but I'm absolutely petrified.

People like me are never going to be the life of the party, but I've stopped thinking of this as a liability. Over the years I've learned to use being an introvert to my advantage. Those of us who hang back rather than work the room shaking hands tend to have gifts that extroverts do not have—most particularly, heightened powers of observation.

On *Say Yes to the Dress: Atlanta*, you may have noticed that I often watch from a distance as a bridal appointment begins. This enables me to monitor the interactions between the bride and her family. I also gauge the personality dynamic within the entourage on the sofa. Who's trying to pull strings by asserting power of the checkbook? Who's biting her tongue? Who's making snarky, passive-aggressive comments about the dress as a smokescreen to camouflage her disapproval of the groom? When a conflict arises, these observations are a big help in figuring out how to resolve it. Generally speaking, I try not to intercede directly. What I do instead is ask open-ended questions that put the group on a path toward working out a solution on their own.

What does this have to do with making friends? "Heightened powers of observation" is just a fancier way of saying that you take in what's going on around you. It's what enables me to recognize almost instantly when a bride has found her dress. Her beaming face, her posture, and the way she carries herself tell me everything I need to know, even if everyone on the couch is too busy squabbling to see it.

Away from the salon, it's what allows me to see people as individuals. It means not only noticing someone's new hairstyle but also sensing when they seem preoccupied. Maybe their eyes are red—have they been crying or burning the midnight oil, or is it an allergy? These may seem like small things, but they are a big part of what helps you understand others and establish and maintain a personal connection.

Be Authentic, Be Vulnerable

Think back to your childhood. As toddlers and preschoolers, we used to be a lot better at making friends than we are now. We confidently put ourselves out there, expecting that other people—both children and adults—would become our friends. Because why wouldn't they? We had no doubt that we were lovable.

Only as we got insulted or snubbed or mocked or bullied did we learn—the hard way—to be less forthcoming and to feel unsure or fearful about how people would respond when meeting us. This defensive approach to human interaction required us to add a layer of emotional armor. We learned to be aloof. When we were adolescents and young adults, our detachment functioned as a flak jacket for the soul, and it was useful because it spared us pain. That protection came at a price, however, because it also "protected" us from forming deeper positive relationships. When I was in school, I wore the label of standoffish or snobby. In reality I was just really shy.

Many of us never took off that flak jacket. Decades later we're still hiding our feelings, but to build meaningful friendships at this stage of life, we have to be willing to shed that protective bulletproof shield and let down our guard. We have to risk presenting our true selves to another person—in other words, we have to dare to be vulnerable.

Vulnerability is one of the keys to friendship and is a particular focus of popular university professor, social worker, and bestselling author Brené Brown. Her TED talk "The Power of Vulnerability" has been viewed by more than thirty-five million people worldwide. "Vulnerability," says Dr. Brown, "is the birthplace of love, belonging, joy, courage, empathy, and creativity." It is essential to connection, what she defines as "the energy that exists between people when they feel seen, heard, and valued; when they can give and receive without judgment; and when they derive sustenance and strength from the relationship."[7]

To me, that's about the best definition of friendship there is.

WHAT'S NEXT
Girlfriends' Guide

- **Friendship Is Vulnerability**

  Being vulnerable is just another term for being open. Have no preconceived notions of who can be your friend. Think like a toddler and put yourself out there—take the risk of being seen. Make the effort to assume the best about people—that they will like you for who you are. Be willing to be seen as less than perfect. Share silly or embarrassing details about yourself—that you love gaudy Christmas sweaters and knock-knock jokes and plastic lawn flamingos and hate the Star Wars movies—all of them. Monte and I love sending each other hilarious photos of our worst outfits from the '70s, just to keep things in check.

- **Friendship Is Nonjudgmental**

  Friends love you when there's nothing lovable about you. When you're at your worst, friends will sit with you and let you be that awful / crabby / angry / distraught / borderline certifiable person for a bit and not think less of you for it. They will love anyway, and when you're ready, those friends will provide the emotional muscle to lift you up and help you find your way back to being your best self.

- **Friendship Is Reciprocal**

  And you need to be willing to do the same for them. Show up, no matter what—it's what friends do. You have to be there when they need you, and you have to understand that there will be occasions when it may be terribly inconvenient for you to do that.

- **Friendship Is Safety**

  You have to be a keeper of secrets and confidences. When a friend confides in you, be her safe place to land, without fear of gossip or judgment.

- **Choose Quality over Quantity**

  Friendship is not a contest—there are no prizes for having the most friends. The goal is to surround yourself with friends who love and support you on your life journey, whether that's a single dear friend or many. I have a small core group of friends, and I'd much rather have a core than an entire apple.

10

Say Yes to Your Best— Your Best Is Yet to Come!

What does it mean to be a success at this point in life? The conventional idea of success is that it's all about money or fame or a title on the door, but I think women have always found that definition to be superficial. We've learned to interpret success as something more deeply personal. Each of us wants to know that we're making a difference in people's lives. Singer-songwriter June Carter Cash put it better than anyone when she said, "I'm just trying to matter."[1]

Looking back, I've done that by motivating and empowering the brides who come into Bridals by Lori. I've helped them look and feel confident as they step into marriage. Looking ahead, I've been thinking more and more about the mothers of the bride and groom who come into my store. When the bride has found her gown and I see the eyes of the moms well up with tears, I know how bittersweet that moment is. Having been both a mother of the bride and a mother of the groom, I know that their emotions are overwhelming, not simply because they are seeing a lovely young woman excited to be on the brink of her future but because they realize that her wedding will be a milestone in their own lives as well.

These women are my tribe, and these are my people. We've already talked about the fact that many of them have been putting themselves last for much of their lives. That attitude not only makes it difficult for them to find their dresses, but after the rice has been thrown and the wedding is over, it makes it hard for them to tackle the life challenges that come next.

Once the nest is empty, there's no one else to put herself last for, and what lies ahead is anything but clear. For me now, my best way to make a difference is by inspiring our generation of women to realize their future potential to the fullest. I want to help women our age embrace their potential and soar. I want that to be my legacy.

If I can do that, I'll leave another legacy as well. Going into this next phase of life, I'm very conscious that I have three sets of beautiful, loving female eyes on me—those of my daughter and my two granddaughters—and I want to make them proud to call me Mom and Bella. I want to be their role model, to lead by example, and to show them that they can do anything they set their sights on.

To me, success has another component as well. It is also about having a sense of contentment, but I don't believe that means being satisfied with what you've already done in life. It's not about resting on your laurels but about being happy with who you are, inside and out. Can you look in the mirror today and like who you see? After my radical double mastectomy, I sure didn't, and there was a time when I wondered whether I'd ever make peace with my reflection.

Pondering my dark circles and my puffy, tired face, it didn't take a lot of soul-searching for me to understand that I was unhappy because I looked bad and felt worse, but another light bulb went on at the same time.

While struggling to recuperate and with a lot of time on my hands, it hit me that I'd lost my self-esteem. When I went looking for it, I found it drooping somewhere down around my ankles, and it was there not just because of how I felt about my appearance. I was miserable because I had a negative attitude, and a lot of that negativity came from being cut off from what I loved.

Sitting around at home, I wasn't making a difference to anybody, and I didn't feel needed. As June Carter Cash might have put it, I didn't matter, and for a while there, I lost my sense of self. I lost Lori.

In the salon, I always knew that my opinion was valued, and I got the daily rush of knowing I was really good at my job. Stuck at home, I didn't have that boost, which only made me appreciate it more.

Heading into this next phase of life, too many of us are starved for praise and validation. It's all too common for us to be overlooked, to not be taken seriously. Younger people tend to believe that our tribe doesn't have opinions worth listening to. Too many are shocked at our competence—at our advanced age, how can we possibly still be good at anything? (Actually, it's a piece of cake.) What we have to do now, girls, is harness our abilities and our experience on behalf of something bigger than ourselves.

Discover Your Purpose

Being sidelined with breast cancer gave me the space and time with God that I needed to address two questions I'd been too busy to ask:

What in my life gives me joy? What gives me a sense of accomplishment and success?

I opened Bridals by Lori in 1980. Starting in a tiny storefront in a small shopping mall, I nurtured my business as it blossomed into a full-service wedding destination that now takes up every square inch of a three-story building. The journey from one to the other was anything but smooth, but even in the roughest patches, I never entertained the notion of giving up and doing something else. The shop has been both joyful and fulfilling. I've been fortunate to be able to make a living with it, and even more blessed that my love for it has never left me. I'm still enthusiastic about what this girl gets to do every day.

And I want *you* to feel this way too! As much satisfaction as I get from my business, I'm still discovering new activities that give me fulfillment. And I'm finding them—in part because of my battle with breast cancer.

Breast cancer is not an equal-opportunity disease. More than half of those affected are women our age, but too many cases are not found in time. There was never a doubt that spreading the word about the lifesaving importance of early detection is valuable work. The surprise to me has been discovering how gratifying it feels to be doing it.

That was a revelation, and now I'm on a mission. I've traveled all over the US and Canada telling my story, but if you'd told me when I was twenty-two that this would be something I'd love doing, I'd have been speechless. (And you know how rare that is.) For me, encouraging women to get regular mammograms is both a calling and a fulfillment. Surviving cancer led me into a deeper understanding of my purpose—I'd been saved, and now I knew there was something God was saving me for.

Today, however, I feel that these breast cancer awareness speeches are just the start of my mission. God still has plans for me, and another door is opening.

One way or another, a lot of women our age are at endings and beginnings. Our *What's Next* time of life will call for us to make life-changing choices and to be hands-on in carrying them out. Going forward into our sixties and beyond, reinvention is inevitable. If you haven't yet discovered an activity that makes you excited to jump out of bed every morning, this is the time to get out and find one.

How do you do that? How do you make the most of what's left of your cookie?

You might start with a little nostalgia. Think back to your younger self. What did you love to do that you don't do anymore? Reflect on the roads not taken and whatever hopes and dreams you've had to abandon or put aside over the years. Did your orthopedic surgeon advise you to stop skiing after you had knee surgery? When your family moved, did you have to leave the piano behind? Even if you no longer dream of conquering the Silver King Trail at Park City, or of playing like Chopin or Billy Joel, try to figure out what it was about those activities that appealed to you.

This is your chance to think about your future. You have an opportunity to create the next phase of your life, but ticktock—your future isn't going to wait forever while you figure stuff out. Now is not the time to leave your dreams on the back burner—you no longer *have* a back burner, so get busy understanding what makes you happy and what gives you a sense of fulfillment. Then make concrete, specific plans that will get you living the life you've imagined. Don't let this next part of your life just happen to you—shape it into what you want it to be. You, girlfriend, are in charge of *What's Next*.

Bloom

The goal is to find your purpose. I was fortunate enough to find mine—well, the first of mine—when I was in my twenties. What if you spent your career in a corporate job? It paid well enough, but now you're wondering, *Was that it? Was that supposed to be my life's work?*

Everyone finds their calling when the time is right. In Jeremiah 29:11 God tells us, "I know the plans I have for you . . . plans to give you hope and a future." There's no age limit in that verse. You can discover your purpose when you're thirty-five, fifty-five, or seventy-five. The point isn't whether or not you're a late bloomer—the point is to bloom, to find your passion in life.

Experiment

In your quest, give yourself permission to fail. It's okay to take a wrong turn, to make mistakes. Not all ideas are good—and not all good ideas are good ideas *for you*. Maybe you've decided to assist in a kindergarten classroom, only to discover that the din of a roomful of five-year-olds makes you crazy. It's surely a worthwhile activity, but if you dread hearing those little voices in the morning, it's not a good fit for you.

You won't have to look far to find a place where you're needed. You just have to discern how your abilities and passion to make a difference dovetail with the needs that are out there. I fell into my love of helping nonprofit organizations by teaming up with Sunshine on a Ranney Day. This amazing 501(c)(3) organization creates handicap-accessible dream rooms for critically ill children. My team and I had the privilege of designing two fairy-tale rooms for little princesses battling childhood cancer.

Another love I've discovered is a therapeutic organization called TurningPoint. This facility played a major role in my post-cancer rehabilitation and is a wonderful resource for women throughout the Atlanta area. Bridals by Lori creates a breast cancer T-shirt every year, and all profits go to TurningPoint. These are just a couple of the causes that have captured my heart.

There are interests that make you feel needed, and there are interests that feed your soul. In this last decade, I've discovered a love for history (which is all Monte's fault!), as well as a passion for antiques, textiles, china, and international travel. My interests and tastes have evolved and changed, and that's what keeps life exciting.

Yours will keep changing too. Don't fear failure. Fear not trying instead. You'll likely explore a number of different activities and interests before making a connection. Find that sweet spot that combines something meaningful with something you love to do.

A Lifetime of Learning

What about that college diploma? There could be a zillion reasons why your university plans got derailed back in the day—maybe you got a raise and a promotion at work and no longer had the time, maybe you found out you were expecting twins, or maybe you just ran out of money.

That's all old news. What's stopping you today? What's standing between you and your BA? I hear some of y'all shaking your heads as you read this, and I know what you're thinking. *If I go back to school, it'll take me five years to get my bachelor's degree. I'll be sixty-seven by the time I graduate.*

Here's my question: Five years from now, if you don't do it, how old will you be?

Follow-up question: If not now, when?

Our brain cells, like the rest of our body, benefit from exercise. Challenging our gray matter—the stuff between our ears, not those gray strands on the top—keeps us intellectually healthy. Continuing education is one of the best ways to stay vibrant and engaged at any age. And it's affordable. Public universities in at least twenty states have established free or discounted tuition for older learners like us. With our wealth of life experiences, we should not be afraid of education.

Even if you don't want to pursue a degree, it's important to keep learning. Educational opportunities are everywhere—you just have to make the effort to find them. Check out your local city and community colleges; they tend to specialize in courses for nontraditional students, and their schedules include classes that meet on the weekend or in the evening, which can be convenient for those of us who are still working.

Many large universities offer extension programs that appeal to mature students. The coursework may be focused on pleasure or scholarship—or both. You can sign up for an exercise class or earn a degree in exercise kinesiology. Take a wine appreciation seminar to help you distinguish your Barolo from your zinfandel and pinot noir, or register for an in-depth lecture series about how climate change is affecting the grape-growing regions of California, France, and Italy. Become a teacher, entrepreneur, personal trainer—just get out there and do something you love.

The Bernard Osher Foundation was established in 1977 and has been a major supporter of higher education for "seasoned" adults ever since. They have established Osher Lifelong Learning Institutes, or OLLIs, at colleges and universities across the country. There are more than four hundred of them so far, and the number keeps growing. From Boise State to the University of Texas to Dartmouth to Auburn (War Eagle!), you'll find courses designed for those of us who are fifty and older.[2]

What about practical instruction, the kind that helps with daily life? If you want to put up a website and are too embarrassed to ask your nephew to teach you how, there are courses for that as well. Udemy (udemy.com) is one of several online learning centers offering a multitude of courses, including coding. Udemy's syllabus includes more than one hundred thousand online course listings. If you don't want to learn how to code, perhaps you'd prefer to learn how to play the guitar instead.

Learn in person or online, for a degree or for the knowledge itself—the point is to explore something that interests you. Whether it's coding or biochemistry or art history or Cajun cuisine, challenge your brain and keep it stimulated—research suggests that making a habit of thinking and learning is far more important that what you learn to think about.

Be a Mentor

One of our most important ways to pay it forward is to use our life experiences to support other women. Maybe you should be giving classes or leading a Bible study, not just attending. Sometimes we don't realize how much we know until someone asks us a question, and then all this information just starts pouring out. Sharing our knowledge is a win-win—it enriches both giver and recipient.

Mentoring is often informal. It can be as casual as showing a granddaughter how to make cookies or teaching her how to identify edible wild plants—and poison ivy—along a hiking trail. Find activities that suit both your enthusiasm and your expertise. I love raising breast cancer awareness, but with my dubious cooking talents, I'm probably not the best cookie-baking mentor. On the other hand, I'd be very good at advising women who are about to launch their own businesses or helping newly graduated young women learn to dress for success as they begin job hunting for the first time.

Some of what you have to share may not be learned but built into your DNA. If you can carry a tune, you can help a child learn to sing. If you grew up knowing a foreign language, you could teach it—or you could teach other native speakers how to improve their English. This doesn't have to take place in a formal classroom setting. It could happen in a community center or a women's shelter, or a juvenile correction facility.

Mentoring is encouragement. It's a powerful force for good because it provides help and support to those who need it most. The gift of encouragement is often the boost that helps someone get to a level that might have taken them years to reach on their own. Churches and agencies like United Way have programs that match mentors with mentees—and often know where the need is greatest.

In the last few years, my friend Elise has poured her heart into ministering to women in the prison system who are about to be released. She provides prayer, encouragement, and support as the women rebuild their lives and prepare to reenter society. Although she's a successful professional, she has discovered her true passion through volunteering, and she now plans to spend her retirement years continuing this important work. Elise is planning her path in a way that makes her feel fulfilled, empowered, and excited for *What's Next*.

Awaken the Entrepreneur Within

I started this book talking about how our tribe is the forgotten demographic, how no one is creating merchandise designed to appeal specifically to women our age. Why not you? You're an expert on the kinds of products you have trouble finding—we could start with clothes and go on from there. If you watch TV, you've already seen too many ads that tend to underestimate us—we're the target market for walk-in bathtubs, salves for warts and arthritis, and disposable underwear for incontinence, but little else.

If you have a background in marketing, or retail, or product development, you know that this is an opportunity staring you in the face. The annals of commercial success are full of stories about entrepreneurs who saw a market that was invisible to everyone else and catered to it. Become an advocate for us in a marketplace where we're ignored and belittled. Fight back when brands demean women in our phase of life. Why can't mature women be represented as fit and fabulous in the media? It's time for things to change.

Do you think you're "too old" to start a business? It depends on whether you're looking at these coming years as the next stage of your life or as the last stage of your life. My dear friend Monte has just opened a fabulous hair salon in Alexandria, Virginia. At the same time, he debuted his new e-commerce line of hair-care products nationwide (who said men weren't good at multitasking?). Monte is in his sixties, and he never thought twice about whether he was too old to pursue this opportunity. Age is not a constraint for either of us, but mindset is everything. The limits others put on us are nothing compared to the limits we are often too ready to put on ourselves. Or as Henry Ford put it, "Whether you think you can, or you think you can't—you're right."[3]

Get Creative

Make room in your life for creativity. It could be painting, or poetry, or gardening, or crafting—whatever sparks your imagination. There is joy in taking simple materials, paints, words, plants, or yarn, and making beauty from them. That joy is twofold—both in the process itself and in seeing the pleasure it brings to others who see it or use it.

One of the activities Mollie loves to do with Brenda, her mother-in-law, is a wine/paint class. Everyone in the group begins with a blank canvas. Looking at the same image, each artist paints her own depiction of it, and it's fascinating to see how distinctly individual the finished canvases are.

What each woman sees and what she chooses to emphasize is different from other women in the group. Perhaps more tellingly, it is also different from the way she might have painted the same subject when she was younger. In effect, she is seeing with the eyes of experience and bringing out shadows, details, and patterns that might have escaped her earlier.

This is what art is supposed to do. Think about some of the most beloved books in children's literature. When kids read Harry Potter, they are caught up in the adventure. As adults, we pick up on so much more, especially the nuances of personal relationships among the characters. When you let your creativity start flowing, it will be the same for you. No matter what you write or paint, you'll have your own history and set of experiences running through your work.

It's not necessary to have any expectation that you might make a living by making art. You don't have to imagine yourself as the next Grandma Moses or Jean Rhys, who wrote *Wide Sargasso Sea*, a prequel to *Jane Eyre* and a bestseller, when she was seventy-six years old. Creativity nourishes the soul, and creative juices are not faucets—they don't turn off when you put down the paintbrush or finish the quilt or the poem. The emotional horsepower you generate when you paint or write or design a garden will spill over and energize other areas of your life as well.

Connect with Nature

Being outside promotes a feeling of well-being in all of us, and there's a natural environment to suit virtually everyone. You could take a month's vacation in a yurt in Outer Mongolia or spend a weekend in a cabin in the Great Smokies, but getting out for an afternoon in the local nature preserve or botanical gardens may also do just fine. How about a nice walk in your neighborhood? I go on two long walks a day with Chloe.

Spending time in the great outdoors makes us feel better and brings a sense of renewal and connection. It's more than just the calming effects of what you see. It's the fresh air on your skin and the warmth of the sun on your back. It's what you hear as well—the cry of seagulls or the sound of a rushing stream or the humorous chattering of squirrels conversing at the park. I have a life philosophy of never missing a sunset when at the beach. Life is just too short to let those gorgeous moments go uncelebrated. As I watch the sun disappear into the Gulf of Mexico, I feel my breathing slow down and my heart fill with gratitude. It is both grounding and stimulating at the same time. It strengthens my connection to God and to this world we share with the other beings he created.

Volunteer

Your world needs you. Pets, wild animals, people, and the earth itself all need the skills you have to offer, and more than anything else, they need your time and your enthusiasm.

Volunteering strengthens your connection with your community—whether it's your church community or your civic community—or both. You'll find activities that will fit your abilities, but you'll also find activities that will expand your abilities to fit their needs.

One of those is Habitat for Humanity, which is one of the most highly respected volunteer-powered philanthropies in the country. They build and repair homes for families in need and often partner with local churches on particular building projects. Habitat is quite aware that construction is often pigeonholed as a man's activity. To counteract that stereotype, they started Women Build almost thirty years ago. Since then, Women Build has been instrumental in helping women learn carpentry, wiring, and other building skills that they can put to use on Habitat projects. There is no age requirement, and no prior experience is necessary.

An organization called Amava is taking a broader approach to engagement. They call it "Discover Your Next," and they partner with a wide variety of organizations to present an evolving portfolio of flexible job and volunteer opportunities. Targeting people entering the post-career phase of life (sound like anyone you know?) and realizing that fulfillment comes in many flavors, they offer many different kinds of experiences, some paid, some not, that include mentoring as well as educational programs, and work with community nonprofit agencies.

These are just a few of many possibilities open to you. It may seem scary to contemplate a future when you're not quite sure what you're going to be doing every day, but it's scarier still to come to a complete stop and then do nothing. To me, nothing could be more frightening than to be on your deathbed and realize you did nothing meaningful with this last phase of life.

WHAT'S NEXT
Girlfriends' Guide

- **Discover Your Purpose and Act On It**

  Set aside time to think about what you want this next phase of life to be, but be aware that you no longer have time for vague aspirations about things you'd like to do "someday." Someday is now, and it's time to get specific. A goal is a dream with a deadline—if you have dreams, either let them go or turn them into an actionable plan.

- **Don't Be Afraid to Fail and Learn from Your Mistakes**

  Imagine different scenarios for your future. Pursue a variety of opportunities. Make mistakes but learn from them. The only person you have to answer to is looking at you in the mirror every morning. Add to your knowledge and your skills. Expect that your interests will grow and change, and make that change your friend. Make challenging your brain a part of your routine. Commit yourself to a lifetime of learning and education. Never stop reading.

- **Open Up**

  Get out of your comfort zone. Put your imagination to work. Make time for artistic expressions. Involve your friends, children, and grandchildren. Get out in nature. Refresh yourself by spending time in nature's open spaces.

- **Surround Yourself with Positive People and Positive Energy**

  Optimism and encouragement are contagious—fill your heart and friendship circle with positivity. Surround yourself with people who are both inspired and inspiring. Tune out negativity—and that includes a constant stream of breaking news. Watching Fox News or CNN all day isn't the best strategy for bringing you peace in the present and hope for the future. Besides, it keeps you indoors.

- **Build Your Legacy**

  Statistics show that this can be the happiest, most rewarding time of life. Be generous with the gifts God has given you. Work toward instilling the best of yourself in others. Participate in improving people and places in a way that benefits your community so that your actions outlive you.

- **Look Ahead**

  Take all you've been through and let yourself be the beneficiary of it all. Embrace this stage of life and kick the fear of aging away. In Haggai 2:9, God tells us that our latter days will be better than our former: "The glory of this present house will be greater than the glory of the former house. . . . And in this place I will grant peace."

Savor Your Cookie

The inspiration for this book was born in the shower, where I was trying to calm down after a young woman at the store asked me how soon I was going to retire. I'd just told her that I was about to turn sixty, and somehow she figured that meant it was time for me to turn out the lights, shuffle out the front door, and move out of the way.

I didn't say anything at the time, but I was offended by the presumption, and the more I thought about it, the madder I got. I have so much wisdom and so much energy left to offer—we all do. This is our time to share the gifts and experiences God has given us. This is also the time for reinvention—for taking those gifts and using them to expand our own horizons. As much as I love the bridal industry, I also know that God has plans for my life outside the store. Empowering women like you and me beyond the aisle is part of the legacy I intend to leave.

I know that there's nothing I can say to that young woman, or to anyone who is convinced that sixty is old—that I'm old—and that therefore I should step aside and let the next generation take over. I can't change what others think of me. I can't stomp my foot and insist that I'm still very good at what I do. I can't make anyone listen to what I have to say. What I *can* do is live out loud, live my best life, and help others do the same.

My plan is to encourage women our age to look ahead, not backward, to expand their possibilities, not narrow them. I want them to start businesses and learn new skills. I want them to become confident handling their own finances. I intend to nag them—nicely, of course—about making time for themselves and about making their health a priority. (Mammograms!) I want to embolden them to become docents at museums and to become civically engaged as board members and commissioners, and as elected officials. And, of course, I want them to be classically but effortlessly well dressed while they're conquering the world.

And no, I have no intention of retiring anytime soon. I'm not about to leave running the salon to someone else, for starters because I can't picture myself sitting around in a La-Z-Boy recliner, wearing clamdigger pants and bad shoes while sipping sweet tea and watching *The View*.

Not going to happen. Not now. Not ever. And I'm as certain of that as I am that God made me a grandmother to reward me for not running away and joining the circus when my kids were teenagers.

That young woman may be sure that I'm over-the-hill, but I'm looking ahead, and I know there's always another mountain. I plan to keep my zest for life and my enthusiasm about the future, even as I'm discovering new interests to explore and be passionate about. That's how I plan to savor the rest of my cookie. If I can do that, I'll prove her wrong, one bite at a time.

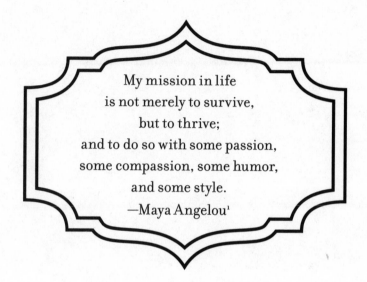

My mission in life
is not merely to survive,
but to thrive;
and to do so with some passion,
some compassion, some humor,
and some style.
—Maya Angelou[1]

Acknowledgments

Thank you to my husband, Eddie. For more than forty years you have encouraged me to embrace my passions and follow my dreams. You have supported me every step of the way as an invested teammate. You are my best friend.

Thank you to my wonderful parents, Jean and Carroll. Your love and unending support, from childhood, to opening the doors of Bridals by Lori, to today have never wavered. You both are my rocks, and I love you dearly.

To my children, their spouses, and my grandchildren, you are the greatest blessings in my life and the gifts that have made all of my hard work worthwhile. I hope I make you proud in all that I do because I do it for each of you. My grandchildren, Caroline, Charlotte, and Jack—I love you so much.

Thank you to my coauthor, Kay Diehl. You immediately understood my vision for this book and the need for this cultural shift. You are a talented writer and an even better friend. Here's to many more literary adventures.

Thank you to my other best friend, Monte Durham. You're always there to lift me up and make me laugh. Your friendship means the world.

Thank you to the entire staff of Bridals by Lori. You are my family. I love each and every one of you, and I am so proud of the strong women we are and what an amazing team we make together.

Thank you to TLC and North South Productions for eleven amazing seasons of *Say Yes to the Dress: Atlanta*. It's been a wild and unforgettable ride. Thank you for believing in me and telling the story of my business.

Finally, thank you W Publishing Group, HarperCollins, and Debbie Wickwire. Thank you for believing in this book, for believing in women over fifty, and for helping spread this important message that the best is yet to come.

Notes

Epigraph

1. Maya Angelou in Juston Jones, "When It Comes to Politics, Friendship Has Its Limits," *New York Times*, July 23, 2007.

Speak for Me

1. Linda Landers, "The Importance of Boomer Women to the U.S. Economy," Girlpower Marketing, accessed March 16, 2020, https://girlpowermarketing .com/the-importance-of-boomer-women-to-the-u-s-economy/.

Chapter 3: One in Eight

1. "U.S. Breast Cancer Statistics," Breastcancer.org, last modified January 27, 2020, https://www.breastcancer.org/symptoms/understand_bc/statistics.

Chapter 4: PMS: The Good Kind, Y'all

1. "Heart Disease," Centers for Disease Control and Prevention, reviewed January 31, 2020, https://www.cdc.gov/heartdisease/women.htm; "Heart Disease in Women," Medline Plus, U.S. National Library of Medicine, National Institutes of Health, updated February 10, 2020, https:// medlineplus.gov/heartdiseaseinwomen.html.

2. "New CDC report: More Than 100 Million Americans Have Diabetes or Prediabetes," Centers for Disease Control and Prevention, July 18, 2017,

https://www.cdc.gov/media/releases/2017/p0718-diabetes-report.html;
"Insulin Resistance & Prediabetes," National Institute of Diabetes and
Digestive and Kidney Disease, National Institutes of Health, May 2018,
https://www.niddk.nih.gov/health-information/diabetes/overview/what
-is-diabetes/prediabetes-insulin-resistance.

3. "Diabetes Hits Women Hard at Menopause: Beat It Back," North American
Menopause Society, accessed March 9, 2020, https://www.menopause
.org/for-women/menopauseflashes/bone-health-and-heart-health
/diabetes-hits-women-hard-at-menopause-beat-it-back.

4. "What Women Need to Know," National Osteoporosis Foundation, accessed
March 3, 2020, https://www.nof.org/preventing-fractures/general-facts
/what-women-need-to-know/.

5. Sharon Brennan-Olsen, "Why Hip Fractures in the Elderly Are Often a
Death Sentence," The Conversation, June 4, 2018, http://theconversation
.com/why-hip-fractures-in-the-elderly-are-often-a-death-sentence
-95784.

6. Kelley Luckstein, "Stephanie Faubion, M.D., Talks Genitourinary
Syndrome of Menopause," Mayo Clinic, December 1, 2017, https://
newsnetwork.mayoclinic.org/discussion/stephanie-faubion-m-d-talks
-genitourinary-syndrome-of-menopause/?mc_id=us&utm_source
=newsnetwork&utm_medium=l&utm_content=content&utm_campaign
=mayoclinic&geo=national&placementsite=enterprise&cauid
=100721; Sherry Ross, M.D., "Treating Vulvo-Vaginal Atrophy," April
20, 2017, https://health.usnews.com/health-care/for-better/articles
/2017-04-20/treating-vulvo-vaginal-atrophy.

7. Lynn Yoffee, "The Link Between Oral Health and Medical Illness,"
Everyday Health, updated November 9, 2012, https://www.everydayhealth
.com/dental-health/oral-conditions/oral-health-and-other-diseases
.aspx; "Gum Disease and Heart Disease: The Common Thread," Harvard
Health Publishing, Harvard Medical School, March 2018, https://
www.health.harvard.edu/heart-health/gum-disease-and-heart-disease
-the-common-thread; Alissa Sauer, "Alzheimer's and Gingivitis: Disease
Linked to Gum Disease," *Our Blog*, Alzheimers.net, April 12, 2019, https://
www.alzheimers.net/alzheimers-and-gingivitis-disease-linked-to-gum
-disease/; "The Connection Between Oral and Mental Health," *Grin!* (blog),
DeltaDental.com, accessed February 27, 2020, https://www.deltadental

.com/grinmag/us/en/ddpa/2017/wellness/oral-and-mental-health
-connection.html.

Chapter 5: God's Grace and Elmer's Glue

1. Amanda Rahn, "Gray Divorce Rate for Couples 50 and Older Doubles in the
   Last Three Decades," Metro Parent, February 20, 2020, https://
   www.metroparent.com/guides/aging/lifestyle/gray-divorce-rate-for
   -couples-50-and-older-doubles-in-the-last-three-decades/.
2. Nancy Gibbs and Michael Duffy, "Ruth Graham, Soulmate to Billy,
   Dies," *Time*, June 14, 2007, http://content.time.com/time/nation
   /article/0,8599,1633197,00.html.
3. Dorothy Parker, "Ballade of Unfortunate Mammals," English Poetry,
   accessed March 16, 2020, https://engpoetry.com/dorothy-parker
   /ballade-of-unfortunate-mammals/.

Chapter 7: Wednesdays with Mom

1. "Projected Doubling of Americans Living with Dementia," Science
   Daily, October 29, 2019, https://www.sciencedaily.com/releases/2019
   /10/191029084315.htm.
2. "Projected Doubling of Americans Living with Dementia," Science Daily.

Chapter 8: Girls Just Wanna Have Funds

1. Ardelle Harrison and Leslie McCormick, *Bank on Yourself: Why
   Every Woman Should Plan Financially to Be Single, Even If She's Not*
   (Georgetown, ON: Milner & Associates Inc., 2019), Kindle, location
   230 of 545.
2. AARP Foundation Finances 50+, "Resources," www.aarp.org/aarp
   -foundation/our-work/income/finances-50-plus-financial-capability
   /financial-resources/.
3. See National Endowment for Financial Education, Smart About
   Money, www.smartaboutmoney.org/.
4. "How the Debt Snowball Method Works," Dave Ramsey, https://
   www.daveramsey.com/blog/how-the-debt-snowball-method-works.
5. See WISER (Women's Institute for a Secure Retirement),
   www.wiserwomen.org/index.php?id=1&page=Home.

Chapter 9: BFF = Better Find Friends

1. Lilo H. Stainton, "Looking to Get to Grips with Loneliness Among NJ's Elderly, Others at Risk," NJ Spotlight, May 31, 2019, https://www .njspotlight.com/2019/05/19-05-30-lawmakers-seek-to-better -understand-loneliness-among-njs-elderly-others-at-risk/.
2. "Social Isolation, Loneliness in Older People Pose Health Risks," National Institute on Aging, April 23, 2019, https://www.nia.nih.gov/news /social-isolation-loneliness-older-people-pose-health-risks.
3. "The 'Loneliness Epidemic,'" Health Resources & Services Administration, last reviewed January 2019, https://www.hrsa.gov/enews/past-issues/2019 /january-17/loneliness-epidemic.
4. Stainton, "Looking to Get to Grips with Loneliness."
5. Mayo Clinic Staff, "Friendships: Enrich Your Life and Improve Your Health," Mayo Clinic, last updated August 24, 2019, https:// www.mayoclinic.org/healthy-lifestyle/adult-health/in-depth/friendships /art-20044860; Jamie Ducharme, "Why Spending Time with Friends Is One of the Best Things You Can Do for Your Health," *Time*, June 25,2019, https://time.com/5609508/social-support-health-benefits/.
6. Janise Hurtig, *Coming of Age in Times of Crisis: Youth, Schooling, and Patriarchy in a Venezuelan Town* (London: Palgrave Macmillan, 2008), 50; Kaitlin Stanford, "These Moms Nail What the True Loneliness of Modern Motherhood Feels Like," Mom.com, September 16, 2019, https://mom.com /momlife/loneliness-motherhood-isolation-friendships.
7. Brené Brown, "The Power of Vulnerability," filmed June 2010 in Houston, TX, TED video, https://www.ted.com/talks/brene_brown_the_power _of_vulnerability?language=en.

Chapter 10: Say Yes to Your Best—Your Best Is Yet to Come!

1. Reese Witherspoon memorably referenced the quote at the 2006 Academy Awards when she gave her acceptance speech as Best Actress for her portrayal of June Carter Cash. June Carter Cash, Quotes, Goodreads, https://www.goodreads.com/quotes/24360-i-m-just-trying-to-matter.
2. For more information go to Bernard Osher Foundation, National Resource Center for Osher Lifelong Learning Institutes, https://sps.northwestern .edu/oshernrc/resources/lifelong-learning/us-lifelong-learning -institute-directory.php.

3. Henry Ford, Quotes, Goodreads, https://www.goodreads.com
   /quotes/638-whether-you-think-you-can-or-you-think-you-can-t-you-re.

Savor Your Cookie

1. Maya Angelou (@DrMayaAngelou), "My mission in life is not merely to
   survive, but to thrive; and to do so with some passion, some compassion,
   some humor, and some style," Twitter, August 19, 2015, 4:18 p.m., https://
   twitter.com/DrMayaAngelou/status/634112210143350784.

About the Author

*L*ori Allen opened Bridals by Lori just two weeks after graduating from the all-female Columbia College in South Carolina. Four decades later she is one of the world's foremost experts on bridal couture and the central figure of TLC's reality show *Say Yes to the Dress: Atlanta*, filmed on-site at Lori's bridal salon and shown in more than 120 countries.

Lori's role as a bridal expert, successful female business entrepreneur, TV personality, and breast cancer survivor has led her to interviews by top-tier media outlets, including CNN, ABC's *Good Morning America*, NBC's *Today*, and the *Wall Street Journal*. She currently resides in Atlanta with her husband, Eddie, and, thankfully, not far from their daughter and her husband, son and his wife, and three grandchildren.

For more information, please visit
SayYesToWhatsNextBook.com